WOODLAND
CRAFT

WOODLAND CRAFT

BEN LAW

First published 2015 by
Guild of Master Craftsman Publications Ltd
Castle Place, 166 High Street, Lewes,
East Sussex, BN7 1XU
In association with Permanent Publications,
The Sustainability Centre, East Meon,
Hampshire, GU32 1HR

This paperback edition published 2017.
Reprinted 2019, 2024

ISBN 978 1 78494 396 7

Publisher Jonathan Bailey
Production Manager Jim Bulley
Senior Project Editor Virginia Brehaut
Managing Art Editor Gilda Pacitti
Art Editor   Rebecca Mothersole
Illustrations Jane Bottomley, Ann Biggs
and Rebecca Mothersole
Cover illustration Celia Hart
Colour origination by GMC Reprographics
Printed and bound in China

All photographs by Ben Law except:
Andrew Perris: 2, 4, 8, 12, 48, 82, 87, 120, 128,
147, 172, 192, 212, 216; F. Morgan: 13; Barn
Carder: 14; Harold Bastin: 89; Graham West: 16
(bottom right); Stuart Whitehead: 22 (bottom left), 23
(top), 135 (centre right); Mike Abbott: 23 (bottom),
177 (right); Rebecca Oaks: 34 (top left); Paul Morton:
28; Hugh Ross: 92 (far right), 94 (centre left); Millar
Hammond: 131 (bottom), 133 (top right), 136; Alistair
Hayhurst: 137; Martin Hazell: 143 (bottom), 146
(bottom right); Eric Oliveira: 204 (bottom left).

FOREWORD

There is a particular pleasure and excitement that comes from holding a handmade object crafted from a living material. Its asymmetries, knots, ripples and elegant inconsistencies seem not flaws but features, speaking of its origins in a wild place and of the work of the individual that formed it. That, on the face of it, is what this book celebrates: the amazing qualities of wood and the things we can do with it.

But it's about much more than that. For the woodland – a world that is spontaneous and natural and, at the same time, utterly subject to our influence – is a microcosm. It has so much to teach us. As Ben Law implies, what goes for one small hazel coppice also goes for the planet. If we care for the woods, they will provide – not just for us but for a host of plants and creatures, from the microscopic to the mighty. Wise woodland management, without which the projects in this book would be impossible, is ecology in a nutshell, if you'll forgive the pun.

I've known Ben for many years, ever since he appeared in my *Cook on the Wild Side* series (and taught me a thing or two about home brewing). He is a pioneer, a quiet campaigner for a more sustainable way of life, whose work has influenced thousands of people. Ben's determination, charm and skill are playing a crucial part in the woodland renaissance we are currently enjoying in the UK. As he points out, woodland skills were all but moribund a few decades ago. Now, thrillingly, the sap is very much rising again, and a new generation of young artisans are turning to the woods once more.

While Ben's work is serious, there is nothing po-faced about this book. His writing, just like his handiwork, is a joyful celebration of wood, in all its flexibility, beauty, colour and strength. *Woodland Craft* is at once traditional and forward-looking. We may have filled our world with man-made fibres, synthetic materials and the products of petroleum, yet woodland and forest remain a living, breathing global fabric that, perhaps more than ever, has a critical role to play in a sustainable future and in the way we build and make things – from the places we live in to the tools we use. If we can husband this resource more wisely, learning from the past but also from the latest science and research, it will spring forward again: an endless, evergreen gift.

The projects that follow are inspiring, and accessible too, whether you want to whittle your own spoons or go as far as constructing a timber-frame caravan. Ben even makes plain the simple joy of splitting well-seasoned logs for firewood, and the technique needed for it.

The very language of these crafts is irresistible: burrs and pollards, adzes and augers, shingles and 'bastard shakes'. That's just one of the things that makes this book such a pleasure to read. But at the heart of it is a thoroughgoing passion and commitment: Ben reminds us what craft truly is. It's not just skill in the making of something, but a knowledge and love of one's materials and an understanding of how the finished piece of work will be seen, appreciated and used: in short, how it will speak to the world.

Hugh Fearnley-Whittingstall

CONTENTS

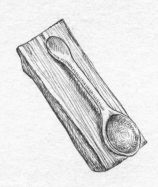

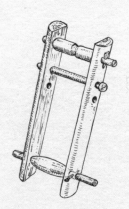

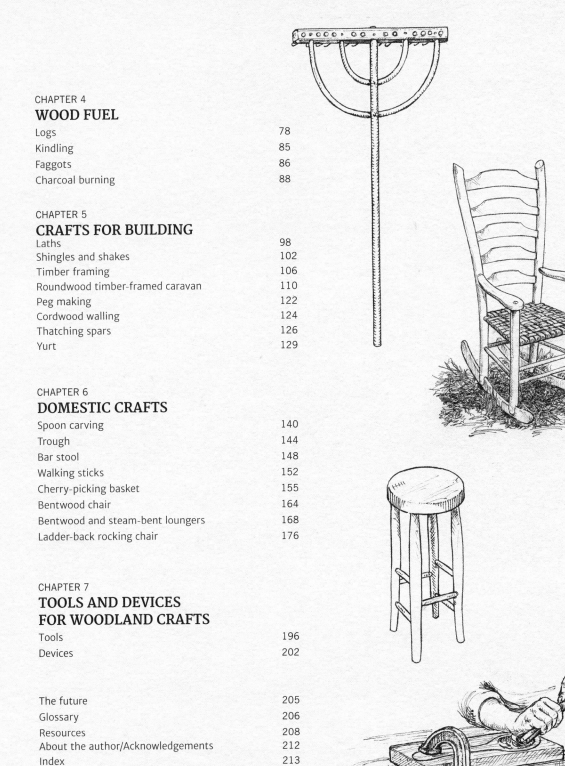

Introduction

As I approach 25 years of living in Prickly Nut Wood, it seems like the right time to focus on the crafts and products that are manufactured from, and in, the woods.

The starting point for all woodland crafts is a sustainable supply of the raw materials needed and, although there are many options for this, none can be more important than good coppice management. This will ensure that future generations have the same opportunities to make and create as we do today.

I am indebted to those who have covered this subject in different ways before me, none more so than Herbert L. Edlin whose book *Woodland Crafts in Britain* (Batsford, 1949) gives a detailed perspective of the vast variety of different crafts that emanated from woodlands prior to the introduction of plastics in the 1950s. Edlin's work catches the moment in time when woodland crafts were beginning to decline. I hope this book shows evidence of their re-emergence.

OPPOSITE PAGE: Woodland track showing overstood coppice to the left and recently cut coppice to the right.

This is predominantly a practical 'how to' book and I hope that by trying some, or all, of the projects you will be able to create a woodlander's life. There are basic shelters, from yurts to a roundwood timber-framed dwelling; chairs and loungers for reclining on; troughs and spoons for your table and two types of fencing for your livestock or garden. As a new generation of woodland craftsmen emerges, new products will be developed to sit with those that have stood the test of time. I welcome the expansion and creativity this brings and look forward to learning from, as well as teaching, the next generation.

The items featured in this book are a mixture of crafts I make myself (I make no excuse for the slight sweet chestnut bias in my choice of materials) and those made by other craftsmen I have visited. In spending time with them as they made their crafts, I was privileged to witness their passion for working with wood and I hope I have managed to convey that to you. My thanks go out to all of them.

THE WOODLAND RESOURCE

Woodland craft materials

The selection of crafts in this book is a mixture of traditional and modern but they all have one main common thread, which is that they are made from green, freshly cut wood.

Poles and prunings straight from the woods form the raw material of woodland crafts. These, together with a selection of specialist tools and handmade devices can help you to discover the world of the woodland craftsman. The enjoyment found in making a chair for your house, crafted with your own hands, an object to enjoy and pass on to future generations is high up in the woodland 'tree of satisfaction'. But to reach the crown of that tree, you must venture into the woods and understand the management and vitality of the raw material you are working with. Labour with love and passion as you work through the cold months of winter, cutting the raw materials to make that chair. It is here in the woods that the woodland craft journey should begin.

Sourcing materials responsibly

There are many sources that can produce the material needed for the projects in this book. Thinnings from broadleaf plantations, stems cut out from hedge laying – or in the city, the variety of different timbers pruned by tree surgeons. All of these can, and should, be used but it is coppice management and the materials it produces that these crafts have evolved from. By sourcing your materials from a well-managed coppice wood, you will be ensuring that the materials are there for future generations. You can find details of where to find local coppiced material on page 209. If you are looking for raw materials to make your craft and do not have the time to cut your own, your local coppice worker is likely to be your most sustainable outlet.

The history of the woodland resource

Wood, a material from trees, grown by the energy of the sun, is the beginning of all crafts and trades. Without wood the blacksmith could not have forged tools, or have handles to hold the tools by. Potters, tanners and glassmakers all needed wood or wood products for their trades.

In fact, our world relied on wood and its uses until the Industrial Revolution in the late eighteenth century. The arrival of coke and, in particular, plastics in the 1950s lead to the demise of many woodland crafts – their role was now outdated. Why carve a bowl out of wood when one can be moulded in plastic every five seconds on a production line? Our oil-based economy has led us blindly towards a faster, more sterile world where individuality and creativity has been bulldozed for rapid production and economic gain with little consideration for the long-term environmental impact.

Woodland crafts originate from a time of need where the skills of the woodsman ensured a ready supply of material to meet the daily needs of life, whether on the farm or in the home. I am not romanticizing the past. One only has to look at the picture from Herbert Edlin's *Woodland Crafts in Britain*, which I refer to as 'the broken man' because of the extreme difficulty of the task he performs. Woodland crafts fortunately no longer ask us to hollow out the end grain of elm logs with an auger to make up water pipes. Such jobs, although needing skill, strength and accuracy, clouded the lines between creativity and drudgery.

After the Second World War many of the coppiced woodlands in the UK fell into decline and the main supply of the raw materials needed for woodland craft was under threat. Returning home from the war, many who had previously worked in the woods moved into the construction industry to rebuild damaged cities, leaving the coppice woods neglected.

Those that entered the woods now were coming from a different approach, that of industrial forestry. They were concerned with producing saw logs and pulpwood predominantly from fast-growing softwoods. The beginnings of this change go back further to the founding of the Forestry Commission in 1919, which was set up to produce more home-grown timber after the First World War. The Forestry Commission has gone a long way towards succeeding in this goal but in doing so has planted a large number of coniferous monoculture plantations on ancient woodland sites.

Now their policy has changed, and conifer plantations are being removed from ancient woodland sites. In many cases the ground flora seedbank has shown good ability to recover, but in some the acidification and shade of the coniferous plantation have negatively affected the biodiversity of the woodland. The growth of interest in continuous-cover forestry seems to offer the best alternative to producing good-quality timber and moving away from the clearfell plantation regimes that are still the dominant forestry pattern in the UK.

'The broken man' using a hand auger to drill through an elm log to make water pipes, Herefordshire, around 1900.

The resurgence of woodland crafts

Although there is still much work to do to regenerate our coppice woodlands in the UK, the past 25 years have seen a small shift towards their recovery. Some woods untouched for 40 or 50 years are now being reworked and, as a result, the interest in woodland crafts is growing. Who could have imagined that a spoon maker would have a shop in Hackney Road, London, making handmade spoons? Or that an event called Spoonfest in England would attract a sell-out crowd as keen individuals converge to refine their skills under the guidance of a new generation of spoon makers? These makers are not just confined to the UK, with specialist spoon makers arriving from Sweden and further afield to share their particular style of craft.

Roundwood timber framing is also attracting global interest and a surge in people wanting to learn the jointing skills. In the US, chair and rustic-furniture makers are on the increase and although they do not have the historic coppice industry and traditions of the UK, individuals and permaculture designers are planting new coppice woodlands as part of their sustainable designs. The increase in the associated crafts will be a natural progression.

Such is the growth of interest in woodland crafts that the variety and diversity, as well as the skill level, are on the increase. Apprenticeships are returning, established makers are training new recruits and the interest in natural building is increasing the demand for shakes, laths and timber frames. My only concern is that with all the positive enthusiasm for making crafts and working wood, the area still needing the most attention is the management of the raw material itself.

ABOVE: *Barn the Spoon at his shop in Hackney, London.*

Woodland management

As I write this it is autumn, the chestnuts are falling from the trees and the rich colours are warming the dewy mornings in the woods. Soon the leaves will fall and once more I will begin my woodland year and head out to cut the coppice. This process, now ingrained in me, is the start of the management cycle that produces the raw materials for these crafts.

Coppicing is the term used to describe the successional cutting of broadleaf woodland during the dormant winter period. In spring, when the sap rises, the stump (known as the stool) sends up new shoots, which are grown on for a number of years until they reach the desired size. They are then cut again during winter and the process repeats itself. The wood cut from coppice is known as underwood and has for centuries supplied a variety of products and supported a large workforce, from the cutter to coppice merchant and craftsman to purchaser.

Coppiced wood is a valuable crop and when managed well can sustain more people per acre than any of the modern forestry alternatives. It is also a sustainable pattern of management, rarely needing any replanting, so the soil is not disturbed and therefore not subject to the risk of erosion. Nutrients are returned mainly through the annual leaf fall.

Coppicing creates a cyclical habitat and a unique ecosystem, and is one of the few patterns of symbiosis known in nature where humans are an important part of the relationship. In a well-managed coppice, the stools are closely spaced, from about 4–6ft (1.2–1.8m) apart and the ground is fully shaded by the leaves and coppice shoots. When it is cut, sunlight pours in, dormant seeds waiting for light emerge and different birds, animals and insect life move into the newly created habitat. Many rare species such as dormice and many types of butterflies are dependent on the coppicing system.

At Prickly Nut Wood the coppice is mainly sweet chestnut; some areas are pure coppice but the majority contain a proportion of standard trees. There are also areas of mixed coppice with standards (large trees growing above the coppice covering a maximum of 15 per cent of the canopy). Oak is the main standard tree with hazel, ash and field maple forming the coppice layer that has been restored from a neglected state and has now re-established a diverse ground flora. This includes a range of key food plants in the life cycle of many butterflies.

Coppicing is currently undergoing a revival and its value as an important landscape feature for social, ecological and commercial value is at last being seen.

ABOVE RIGHT: A derelict coppice wood needing recutting.
RIGHT: Re-emerging chestnut coppice at Prickly Nut Wood.

THE BASICS OF SUCCESSFUL COPPICE MANAGEMENT

- Cut a minimum of $1/3$ acre (0.135 hectare). Any less will not allow enough light in for good-quality regrowth A larger area is preferable.
- Leave a few standard trees if they exist, or encourage new ones. A coppice with standards is more diverse than pure coppice.
- If there are lots of standards, reduce the canopy cover to 10–15 percent. This will allow enough light to ensure the coppice regenerates well.
- Leave some standing deadwood for wildlife habitat.
- Deer will need to be controlled, by fencing or stalking.
- Increase the stocking rate by replanting or layering.

ABOVE: Cutting is finished for the year. Products are bundled to the left; note the charcoal kiln (centre) and cleaving brake just visible beneath oaks (right).

OPPOSITE PAGE
TOP LEFT: Abundant chestnut coppice at Prickly Nut Wood.
TOP RIGHT: Coppice in winter.
CENTRE: A good deer fence ensures coppice regrowth.
BOTTOM LEFT: Sorting chestnut coppice into craft material.
BOTTOM RIGHT: The rare pearl-bordered fritillary butterfly, once common in coppice woodlands and reliant on coppicing to create a suitable habitat for it to live.

DIRECTORY
OF TREE SPECIES

Coppiced alder showing good-quality, straight poles.

Alder *(Alnus glutinosa)*

Description and characteristics

The leaves are alternate, rounded and dark green with a slightly serrated edge. The bark is dark brown and rough in texture and often sprouts new growth near the base.

One of the unique qualities of alder is the ability to provide nitrogen by absorbing it through the air and then fixing it into the root nodules through a relationship with the ascomycetes fungus *Frankia*. The nitrogen is then drawn up into the leaves and when the leaves fall in autumn and then decompose, the nitrogen is made available to other tree and plant species through soil enrichment. Another unique quality of alder is the bright orange colour it turns when freshly cut; sadly this fades to a light reddish-brown colour when dried.

Flowers and fruit

The purple catkins and buds are distinctive and make the tree easy to identify in winter. Male and female catkins grow on the same tree and pollination is by the wind.

Habitat

The site of the common alder growing in a woodland often marks a wet site. Alder favours stream banks and damp soil conditions, where it thrives. Alder is able to spread downstream by its cleverly evolved seed, which is designed to float for considerable distances before becoming washed into a bank, where it will happily establish.

Distribution

The common alder *(Alnus glutinosa)* is widely distributed across Europe from Scandinavia to southern Greece. It can also be found in northern Africa, parts of Asia and Siberia. It has been introduced into the US, Canada, New Zealand, Australia and South Africa.

Ecological value

Alder is a food plant for many caterpillars of both moths and butterflies and for the larvae of invertebrates like caddis flies and water beetles. It provides winter food for birds, including goldfinches, from its seed. Alder's ability to thrive in wet conditions and the ability to fix nitrogen are key to its ecological value.

Coppice notes

Alder coppices well and produces straight, fast-growing poles.

Uses

Alder has been traditionally used for clog soles, turnery, carving, broom heads, underwater revetments and charcoal. As alder grows in wet conditions, it is often difficult to extract but by converting it to charcoal, the resulting charcoal is only one fifth of the weight of the original timber and therefore easier to extract. The sapwood and heartwood are difficult to tell apart and the wood will work easily with hand tools and is sought after for turnery. The wood is perishable but has the ability to dry very fast, with little movement. An air-dried 1in (25mm)-thick plank will have dried to 15–20 per cent moisture content in six months.

LEFT: Distinctive purple catkins.
RIGHT: The vibrant colour of freshly felled alder.

Ash *(Fraxinus excelsior)*

TOP: The finished crown of a yurt – 'eye to the heavens'.

ABOVE: Ash bow-making workshop, Brookhouse Woods, Herefordshire.

TOP LEFT: A mature ash in midsummer.

TOP RIGHT: Mixed ash and hazel coppice being worked at Prickly Nut Wood.

BOTTOM LEFT: Ash yurt crowns being steam bent.

BOTTOM RIGHT: Coppiced ash at Prickly Nut Wood.

Description and characteristics

The distinctive leaves of the ash tree have a long stalk that ends with a terminal leaflet, while the other leaflets are in opposite pairs. They are oval with a toothed edge (9–13 leaflets on each stalk is usual). The bark is a greenish grey in colour and smooth while the tree is young but then fissures with age.

Flowers and fruit

The flowers of ash appear at the same time, or just before, the leaves break. They are green, tipped with purple in appearance and can be male or female on the same tree.

In winter, ash has dark, almost black, buds that help to distinguish it. Its seeds, known as keys, will often hang on the trees into winter.

Habitat

Ash grows on many types of soil but succeeds best in chalk or limestone soils where it will seed freely.

Distribution

The European ash is a widely distributed native tree across Europe with the exception of northern Scandinavia. It has been introduced to New Zealand, Canada and parts of the US. In the UK and across much of Europe, ash is currently under threat from *Chalara fraxinea* (ash dieback), which may have a significant impact on the volume of material that is available to craft workers in the future.

Ecological value

Ash supports a large number of invertebrates and caterpillars of moths and butterflies. More than 500 species of lichen have been recorded on ash trees in the UK. Ash is late to come into leaf and casts a light shade, so ash woods benefit ground flora and natural regeneration.

Coppice notes

Ash grows well in a mixed coppice or as a standard tree above coppice as its compound leaves cast a light shade. I grow ash in a mixed coppice with hazel, where the hazel is cut on a 7-year cycle and the ash on a 21-year cycle. This allows the ash to get to a more useful size for many of the craft products for which it is sought. As ash comes into leaf late, and only casts a delicate shade, the hazel will tolerate its longer cycle.

Uses

Ash has a wide tradition of craft uses from tool handles to furniture and is a favourite wood for many contemporary greenwood chair makers. Hay rakes, tent pegs, yurts, bows and oars are all commonly made from ash as are many sports equipment items like hockey sticks and snooker cues. Ash is a non-durable timber so its craft purposes are mainly for items that are used or stored inside or else a preservative is applied, such as varnish for oars. It cleaves well and is a good timber to work with a draw knife or chisel. There is no distinctive heartwood in ash but faster-grown stems are favoured for their strength by craftsmen. Older stems often suffer from a 'black heart', making the wood known as 'olive ash', which is highly sought after by wood turners and some furniture makers. One special quality of ash is its high resistance to shock loading, making it the chosen wood for tool handles in Europe as hickory is in the US.

Beech *(Fagus sylvatica)*

Description and characteristics

Beech leaves are oval, alternate with pairs of parallel veins. In spring they are a vivid light green with tiny white hairs, darkening to a mid-green colour throughout summer before changing through yellowy gold to orange/brown in the autumn. The bark is smooth and grey and the tree is usually buttressed at the base. The buds are long, slender and brown and are set alternately on thin twigs. In appearance it is hard to differentiate the sapwood from the heartwood and the colour is usually a pale brown. It is straight grained and often flecked.

Flowers and fruit

The flowers are wind pollinated and appear after the leaves. The male flowers are yellow and on long stalks while the female flowers are a greenish white and appear closer to the stem. The seeds (known as beech nuts) appear in hairy brown husks in autumn and open into four lobes usually to reveal two triangular seeds.

Habitat

Beech prefers well-drained chalk and limestone soils.

Distribution

Beech is distributed widely across southern, western and central Europe, as far as southern Scandinavia and is found in profusion in the Chiltern Hills and over the North and South Downs in the UK.

TOP: *Looking up into a clump of beech trees.*

BOTTOM: *Distinctive case that covers the beech nuts.*

Ecological value

Beech is recorded to support 94 species of invertebrates and provides food for birds and small mammals through its seeds. Jays have been known to plant the seeds hence enabling the spread of the species.

Coppice notes

Beech is not usually coppiced due to its slow speed of regrowth and the higher risk of it being grazed off by browsing animals. It is more commonly pollarded to overcome this.

Uses

Craft uses for beech are carving, spoons, bowls, toys, broom heads and tent pegs. Beech, when grown larger and sawn, is also used for a wide range of furniture items.

Spalted beech is popular amongst carvers and turners. The wood is reasonable to work with hand tools. Care must be taken when drying beech as it is prone to cup (warp) and split. Beech is non-durable. Traditional bodgers lived out in the woods, cleaving and then turning beech into chair legs, which then supplied the Windsor chair makers among others.

Birch (silver birch, *Betula pendula*, and downy birch, *Betula pubescens*)

Betula pendula

Birch remaining graceful after a heavy snowfall.

Flowers and fruit

The flowers are formed of male and female catkins that appear on the same tree. The male catkins are a purple/brown in colour and dangle down whereas the green female catkins are pale green and more erect. They open in spring. After leaf fall the catkins break up and distribute many tiny windborne winged seeds, which distribute themselves widely and account for the birch's pioneering reputation.

Habitat

Both types of birch are colonizers of poor soils and their leaf fall helps improve soil conditions over time. The downy birch will thrive on wetter sites than the silver birch.

Distribution

The silver birch and the downy birch are both native to the British Isles and across much of Europe. Birch can be found as far north as Lapland, and slow-growing birch forests are a feature within the Arctic Circle. No other broadleaf tree can survive so far north.

Ecological value

Birch has an open canopy that allows light to penetrate and this benefits many flowering plants and mosses. Birch is known to support 334 species of invertebrates and is an important tree for many birds, providing winter food from its catkins.

Description and characteristics

The leaves of the silver birch are alternate and shiny with ragged edges and a straight base. The downy birch looks similar but the edges are more even and the base is triangulated and thin. The bark of the silver birch is reddish in colour, becoming silver white with black flecks while the downy birch bark is a reddish brown but can occasionally look more like the silver birch. The wood is a creamy-white colour and there is no obvious colour distinction between the sapwood and the heartwood.

LEFT: *Peeling birch bark to use for lighting fires.*

CENTRE: *Birches being tapped for the fast-flowing sap in early spring.*

BELOW: *Native American birch basket with spruce-root stitching.*

Coppice notes

Birch can be coppiced while it is young, but older trees often fail to regrow. This is rarely a problem as birch casts a lot of seed and is a fast-growing pioneer in the establishment of new woodlands and the re-establishment of secondary woodland. The tree will rarely live longer than about 80 years in the British Isles.

Uses

In northern countries where the choice of trees and wood for craft work is more limited than the large selection I am blessed with in the south of England, birch has many uses, from basketry to floorboards and jewellery to bark canoes.

The wood is pleasant to carve and turn and has a particularly attractive figure when spalted. Birch is commonly used for kitchen treenware and children's toys. The wood is perishable, though the bark is the most durable part and is harvested for a wide range of craft produce. The bark is usually harvested from freshly felled trees when the sap is flowing in early spring; however careful peeling of the bark without disturbing the cambium layer will allow the tree to live and grow a secondary bark to replace what has been harvested. The harvesting of bark from living trees is most successfully carried out on paper birch (*Betula papyrifera*) native to Canada and the US. Birch bark is highly flammable and, when freshly peeled, it is a great fire starter. The fast sap flow of birch in early spring can be collected – a gallon can be obtained in a few days and makes a fine country wine.

LEFT: *The flammable bark makes the perfect fire starter.*

Cherry *(Prunus avium)*

Description and characteristics

The leaves are elliptical, alternate with a pointed tip and forward-pointing teeth. The stalk is long and red. The leaves turn a crimson red in autumn. The bark is purple/brown, shiny and has horizontal bands that peel in horizontal strips. The heartwood is darker than the sapwood with a reddish-brown colour and it is a straight-grained timber with moderate durability.

Flowers and fruit

The European cherry stands out in spring when its white blossom is an early arrival of colour amongst the woods. The flowers are insect pollinated and form small red cherry fruits, which are eaten by birds who pass the woody seed and help distribute the tree.

Habitat

The wild cherry does especially well on clay soils over chalk and is often seen established amongst beech woods on the chalk hills in the south of England.

Distribution

The wild cherry is distributed widely across Europe, as far north as Denmark. The rootstock is used widely for the grafting of improved fruit varieties and this has aided its domestic distribution.

Ecological value

Wild cherry supports a large number of insects and caterpillars of moths and butterflies. The spring blossom is an important nectar source for bees and the resulting cherries are an important food source for many species of birds.

LEFT: The white blossom from a cherry grove in ancient woodland.

ABOVE: The distinctive bark of European cherry.

Coppice notes

Cherry suckers from the root, rather than coppices from the stump, and groves of wild cherry of similar age are often found in woods that have been worked to produce materials for woodland crafts.

Uses

Cherry steam bends well and is good to work with hand tools. It is a popular wood for furniture making, turnery and carving. It could be used as an alternative to ash in the ladder-back chair project in this book (see page 176) and for the bar stools (see page 148), spoon (see page 140) and trough carving (see page 144).

Elm *(Ulmus procera)*

Description and characteristics

Elm leaves are round to oval in shape, alternate and are on average 3in (75mm) long. The edges are double-toothed with a rounded tip. The upper surface feels rough. The bark is greyish brown.

Flowers and fruit

The flowers are formed in small clusters and appear before the leaves. They are dark pink to purple in colour and both male and female parts are contained within the same flower. The seeds are winged and wind distributed.

Habitat

Primarily a hedgerow tree, it likes open conditions and prefers fertile soils. It has a good tolerance to salt air.

Distribution

The distribution range is across southern and eastern Europe. Dutch elm disease was first identified in the Netherlands and entered the UK in 1967. The disease is spread by the scolytid beetle that burrows under the tree bark and carries a fungus. It spreads the fungus, which in turn kills the tree. Once the dominant tree of the English landscape, the English elm now resides, under close observation, as a street and parkland tree in Brighton where it continues to thrive.

Ecological value

Birds feed on the seeds. The elm also supports caterpillars and butterflies. The decline of the English elm has affected the population of white lesser hairstreak butterflies.

Coppice notes

Elm does not coppice but suckers. Most management now involves the wych elm, predominantly in northern England and Scotland.

Coils of wych elm bast on a ladder-back chair with a woven wych elm seat.

Uses

Elm has such a history of use for crafts in the British Isles that, despite the English elm's virtual eradication due to Dutch elm disease, the wood as a commodity is still in circulation and other species such as the wych elm (*Ulmus glabra*) are gaining popularity amongst craftsmen. Wych elm bast (the layer of 'inner bark' between the cambium layer and the bark) is becoming popular as a woven seating material and wych elm wood is being used as a replacement for English elm seats. The heartwood is a reddish-brown colour with irregular grain, which produces an attractive figure, visible in the seats of many country chairs.

It is a challenging wood to work with hand tools due to its irregular grain pattern but has been traditionally used for cabinets, chairs, flooring, coffins, weatherboarding and veneers. The wood is not durable but rarely splits and hence has been used as partitions in stables and livestock sheds where the boards are liable to be kicked. It was the wood of choice for wheel hubs and was painstakingly bored out with a long-handled auger for water pipes (see page 13). Elm, when kept soaked with water, is more durable than when exposed to the air and dampness, hence its use for water pipes and underwater gates, groynes and pilings.

ABOVE: Coppiced hazel showing rods growing for hurdle making.
RIGHT (TOP): A flush of primroses appear where the hazel coppice has been cut.
RIGHT (CENTRE): Twisted hazel.
RIGHT (BOTTOM): Hazel catkins emerging in the heart of winter.

Hazel *(Corylus avellana)*

Description and characteristics

Hazel leaves are broad with a short tip, alternate and with toothed edges. The surface is hairy. The buds are brown in winter, turning green by early spring. The bark is light brown to grey and fairly smooth, but there are many regional variations of hazel.

Flowers and fruit

Hazel is monoecious, meaning that both male and female flowers are found on the same tree. The male flowers, which appear before the leaves, are long yellow pendulous catkins. The female flowers are small and crimson and often missed with the naked eye. Wind pollination ensures formation of their fruit, the hazelnut.

Habitat

Hazel can be found from woodlands to hedgerows across much of the United Kingdom. In woodlands it is often found in mixed coppices with ash, field maple and hawthorn.

Distribution

Hazel is widely distributed across Europe with the exception of Mediterranean regions. It was one of the first trees to recolonize Britain after the last ice age according to pollen analysis. Although hazel will be found in many types of soil, it is in the chalk uplands of the southern English counties of Dorset, Hampshire and Wiltshire where the best-quality hazel copses can be found.

Ecological value

Hazel is valuable for wildlife. The leaves provide food for many species of moth such as the large emerald and nut-tree tussock moth. It is the favoured habitat of dormice, who rely on the nuts to fatten themselves up prior to going into hibernation. When grown as a coppice, the environment is a favoured habitat for the fritillary species of butterfly and many wildflowers such as the early purple-flowering orchid, primrose and bluebell.

Coppice notes

Hazel historically was the 'go to' wood of the countryside. Every village would have areas of hazel coppice and associated craftsmen to make the day-to-day artifacts needed for rural life. In Edlin's *Woodland Crafts in Britain*, he mentions a statute passed by Edward IV in 1483 authorizing the enclosure of woods for a term of seven years after cutting. Hazel is traditionally cut on a seven-year cycle and this level of protection shows the value and importance of hazel coppice through history. Grown as a single-species coppice, sometimes with oak standards, these productive coppices produce quality hazel rods for a wide range of craft produce. I have visited some of the finest hazel copses at Cranborne Chase and King's Sombourne in southern England where the cutting rights are closely guarded by coppice workers who know the value of the woodlands they work.

Uses

The uses of hazel are many and from region to region this adaptable wood has been utilized for a vast range of products. Hazel's usefulness lies in its ability to cleave easily and, when twisted, the fibres will separate to form a strong rope. This twist allows the wood to be turned back on itself and it is this quality that has been used for generations to make wattle hurdles.

From sheep hurdles to thatching spas, walking sticks, pea sticks, beanpoles, faggots, fish traps, animal traps, etherings, barrel hoops, cradles, creels and crates for the potteries, the craftsman has turned to hazel. Many of these traditional products have been replaced with plastic alternatives, but for a number of these products hazel is still the first choice.

Spars for thatching are still made primarily from hazel, although I have come across a few sweet chestnut spar makers in the southeast of England where chestnut copses outnumber hazel.

The garden market has made sure that the wattle hurdle continues to be popular. Now rarely used for sheep penning, it is mostly used as a woven garden fence. Other common garden structures such as obelisks and plant supports, trellises and pea sticks all continue to support the management of hazel coppices and the craftsmen who work them.

Lime *(Tilia cordata)*

Description and characteristics

The leaves of the lime are heart shaped but the two lobes are rarely of an even size. They are alternate, toothed and shiny on top. The leaves first appear pale green in colour and then darken to a deeper green. The bark is smooth and grey. Lime, in particular the small-leaved lime as this is the tree that is most often found in coppice woods in England, is a pale yellowy-white wood that darkens slightly to a pale brown over time. The American lime (*Tilia americana*) known commonly as basswood has similar properties.

Flowers and fruit

The clustered flowers arrive from the middle of June and are greenish/yellow in colour. Each flower has its own stalk and the clusters of seven or eight have a main stalk. The seeds ripen in the autumn and fall as small rounded balls.

Habitat

Lime was one of the dominant tree species in southern and eastern England 4,000 years ago. It forms extensive woods of mixed broadleaf.

Distribution

Widespread across northern Europe, central Scandinavia, central Russia and south as far as central Spain, Italy, Greece and into western Asia.

Ecological value

Lime trees provide food for moth caterpillars and are favoured by aphids, which in turn provide food for ladybirds and hoverflies. The flowers are a very good nectar source for bees.

Coppice notes

Small-leaved lime (*Tilia cordata*) coppices well. Ancient small-leaved lime coppice woodlands can be found in eastern England.

Uses

Lime is used for all forms of wood carving and is closely associated with Grinling Gibbons, whose decorative carving can be found in St Paul's Cathedral (London) and near to me at Petworth House (West Sussex).

It is still favoured as a carving wood as it resists splitting in any cutting plane and is easy to work with both machine and hand tools. It is also used for musical instruments, toys, turnery, beehives and decorative veneers. Lime is a non-durable timber but contains a strong bast, which like wych elm is used for seat weaving. The timber can distort when drying, basswood is more stable. The leaves when young make a fine salad and the flowers a popular herbal tea.

FAR LEFT: The distinctive shape of the lime leaf.

LEFT: A small-leaved lime growing at Prickly Nut Wood.

Oak (pendunculate oak, *Quercus robur* and sessile oak, *Quercus petraea*)

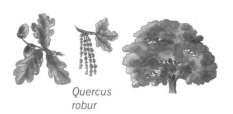

Quercus robur

Removing my cap in awe of the Queen Elizabeth Oak, Cowdray Park, Midhurst, West Sussex.

Description and characteristics

Oak leaves are easy to distinguish as they are alternate and have a wavy outline, made up of an irregular shape of lobes on each side. The pendunculate oak has almost no stalk to its leaves with a small set of lobes at the base of the leaf, whereas the sessile oak has a clear stalk. The bark on both is fissured and grey in colour. One of the beautiful characteristics of oak is the rays, sometimes referred to as 'silver grain', which give the timber such an attractive figure when quarter sawn. Oak is very durable and the high tannin content means it will corrode ferrous metals. It is dense and hard and is difficult to work with hand tools unless it is green.

Flowers and fruit

The flowers appear at the same time as the leaves, usually early May. The male flowers are similar in both species and hang down as catkins. The female flowers occur at the tips of the young branches. The female flowers of the pendunculate oak appear on a stem and the female flowers of the sessile oak are stalkless. The fruit (acorns) naturally follow the pattern of the female flowers with acorns on the pendunculate oak appearing on stalks and those on the sessile oak appearing without.

Habitat

Oak is tolerant of most soils, in particular clay soils and sandy loams.

Distribution

With the loss of so many elms in the UK, oak is often the tree associated most with the British landscape. Two native species that are widespread across the UK are the pendunculate oak and the sessile oak. These oaks are common through much of Europe from southern Scandinavia to the Mediterranean.

Ecological value

Oak supports 334 species of insect and over 300 species of lichen. The roots have many mycorrhizal relations with many species of fungi. It is visited by numerous species of birds and moths and butterflies feed off it and make their habitat around it. The purple emperor butterfly likes the oak canopy while the purple hairstreak butterfly feeds exclusively on oak leaves.

Coppice notes

Oak can be coppiced but the regrowth is slow and unpredictable. It is more commonly grown as a standard tree above hazel or mixed coppice, or grown as a plantation timber.

Uses

The strength and durability of oak has many uses, from timber-frame houses to the great warships of the navy. In Cumbria, there is still a small market for oak poles that are peeled for bark to be used in the tanning industry. Tannic acid in the bark preserves the hide and leaves the leather flexible and durable. The bone-like poles are then used for making various items. However, unless the oak has grown very slowly, the lack of sapwood can reduce the lifespan of such projects – but one makes use of what is locally available.

I grow oak at Prickly Nut Wood primarily as a standard tree above the coppice and convert the better-quality timber to planks for furniture making. Poorer trees are sawn 'through and through' (milling the timber into boards with the bark still on both edges) and left to air dry for 5–6 months before being kiln dried for floorboards, doors and window frames. Poorer quality still is used for cladding and fencing.

RIGHT: Oak fencing from Prickly Nut Wood. The frame is sawn oak post-and-rail and the laths are sawn on a mobile sawmill, 5/32in (4mm) thick. The round zales are sweet chestnut. The oak is sawn green and the fence tightens as it shrinks.

TOP (LEFT): Peeled oak bark, ready to supply to the tannery.

TOP (RIGHT): Oak dining table at Prickly Nut Wood.

ABOVE: Oak that has been sawn 'through and through' air drying before being kiln dried.

LEFT: An oak window frame and waney-edged oak boarding.

Sweet chestnut
(Castanea sativa)

LEFT: *Chestnuts opening for harvest.*

BELOW: *Heartwood of sweet chestnut: the cream-coloured ring around the outside is the sapwood.*

Description and characteristics

The leaves are large (sometimes up to 10in/25cm in length), oval and alternate with saw-edged teeth and parallel veins. The bark is grey/brown and smooth when young, but soon develops deep fissures and a distinctive spiral pattern with age.

Flowers and fruit

Sweet chestnut is a late-flowering tree with the flowers usually not appearing until July. Unusually, both the male and female flowers appear on the same stalk. The flowering stems, which resemble long yellowish catkins, hang down. The male flowers, formed of six bracts made up of seven flowers, are spaced at intervals along them. The female flowers are formed near the base of the stalk. They are small, green, oval and hairy with three flowers in each. They are wind and insect pollinated (the musty smell emitted helps attract insects) and the seeds (nuts) develop fast. The nuts continue to develop in a spiky case that splits open to reveal three nuts in autumn when they are ripe.

Habitat

Now naturalized amongst Britain's broadleaved woodlands, sweet chestnut is primarily grown as a coppice crop. It prefers a slightly acidic sandy loam but dislikes waterlogged or alkaline soils and exposed sites.

Distribution

Native to southern Europe, sweet chestnut is considered to have been introduced into Great Britain by the Romans primarily as a food source. However, recent evidence suggests it may have been established prior to the Roman arrival. Either way, this fast-growing, durable tree is now the main commercial coppice species in Great Britain.

Ecological value

Sweet chestnut has a large number of good fungal associations. Chestnut supports a number of butterfly and moth species. When grown as a coppice-with-standards system instead of pure coppice, diversity of wildlife is greatly increased.

Working chestnut coppice in winter.

Coppice notes

Sweet chestnut, as a coppice system, is primarily grown across the southeast of England where 46,950 acres (19,000 hectares) are currently available. Sweet chestnut has the ability to produce heartwood at a very young age, often with only three years' growth of sapwood. This enables it to produce durable heartwood in a very small diameter pole.

Single-species chestnut coppices cut on a 16-year rotation can produce between 50 to 70 tons of greenwood material per acre. This is a plentiful supply of material for the craft industry. CD Begley's Forestry Commission report of 1955 broke down plots by the acre and analysed the range of craft produce produced. A one-acre (0.4 hectare) plot of 16-year-old sweet chestnut coppice produced 1,679 cleft posts, 26,875 pales, 575 pea sticks and 7.1 cords of firewood. At today's prices that would bring in approximately £8,000 per acre every 16 years, equating to £500 per acre, per annum.

Uses

The durability of the sweet chestnut, aligned with its ability to cleave very readily, makes it a well-used, versatile wood for craftwork – particularly for fencing and garden products. Sweet chestnut is the main timber species at Prickly Nut Wood where I work and I am able to make and supply a wide range of products from this valuable coppice. The table below illustrates the variety of items it is possible to make from different rotations of sweet chestnut.

USES FOR SWEET CHESTNUT COPPICE

Age	Use
3 years	Walking sticks, faggots
5 years	Walking sticks, faggots, yurt poles, hedging stakes, beanpoles, pea sticks, pegs, woven panels, straw bale spikes, balustrades, rustic furniture
7–12 years	Rustic furniture, laths, pales, rose arches, gate hurdles, trellis panels, trug handles
20 years	Laths, pales, rustic furniture, charcoal, firewood, barrels, bird tables, fencing posts
30+ years	Roundwood timber framing, post-and-rail fencing, fencing posts, decking, cladding, arbours, gates, shingles, window frames, charcoal, firewood

Salix viminalis

Willow (pussy willow, *Salix caprea* and osier willow, *Salix viminalis)*

LEFT: Pussy willow awakens bees to spring.

RIGHT: Rustic willow basket with a twisted rope-style handle.

Description and characteristics

Pussy willow has broad oval leaves, which are alternate and have a short point. The edges have small teeth and the leaves are grey/green in colour. The bark is smooth and grey with fissures appearing at the base with age. *Salix viminalis*, the common osier (one of the main basket-making trees) has long narrow leaves which are green on top and silvery beneath with hairs. They are toothless, sharp-pointed and the edges roll inwards towards the under side.

Flowers and fruit

Willows are dioecious, meaning they produce male and female flowers on different trees. The male catkins of the pussy willow are upright, grey and hairy at first then turning yellow. The female catkins are longer and are silvery green. Osier willows have similar flowers.

Habitat

Willows enjoy wet and damp locations with neutral to alkaline soils.

Distribution

Pussy willow is distributed through central and eastern Europe, while the osier willow is distributed from central Europe to western Asia.

Ecological value

Pussy willow provides the first nectar flow in spring for bees in the woods. There are large numbers of insects associated with willows, in particular moths. The sallow clearwing, sallow kitten and puss moth visit the goat willow and the lackey, herald and red-tipped clearwing the osier willow. Goat willow is also the main food plant for the purple emperor butterfly.

Coppice notes

Osier willow is harvested annually by coppicing to provide basket-making rods. They are usually grown in purpose-made beds that provide the longest, straightest rods for basketry. Almond willow (*Salix triandra*), purple willow (*Salix purpurea*) and osier willow (*Salix viminalis*) are some of the main varieties grown for this purpose.

Uses

The native pussy, grey and white willow have limited uses for crafts. Willow has been the favoured wood for basket making for many years due to its flexible long rods and, although all these species are useable, it is the osier willows that are best. White willow is fast drying and non-durable but works well with hand tools. Traditional uses are cricket bats (made from *Salix alba* var. *caerulea*), sieve frames, trugs, crates and baskets.

Osier willow beds for basketry, as part of a wetlands system.

CRAFTS FOR
FARM AND GARDEN

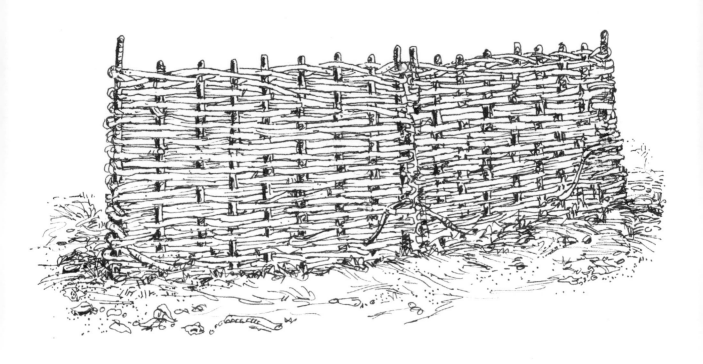

WATTLE HURDLE

Dating back to Neolithic times where they were used laid down as a primitive trackway in the south-west of England, wattle hurdles have a history of craftsmanship that has evolved over generations. The wattle hurdle is a lightweight protective panel used by shepherds (who could carry four at a time) for folding sheep as they controlled access to grazing. These hurdles offered protection at lambing time from wind and driving snow. Today they are used largely as attractive panels in gardens, for perimeter fencing or screening an unsightly object. The hurdle is a beautiful craft object, made without the need for nails or fixings.

Materials you will need

1 plank for the mould: 7ft (2.1m) long x 3in (75mm) thick x 7in (178mm) wide

2 hazel rods for the end zales: 1¼in (31mm) diameter (these should be 6in/150mm longer than your chosen height for the hurdle)

4 hazel rods for intermediate zales: 1½in (38mm) diameter (these should be 6in/150mm longer than your chosen height for the hurdle)

4 hazel rods for bottom rods: 7ft (2.1m) long x ¾in (19mm) diameter

2 hazel rods for bottom rods: 9ft (2.7m) long x ¾in (19mm) diameter

1 hazel rod for top rods: 4ft (1.2m) long x ¾in (19mm) diameter

1 hazel rod for top rods: 8ft (2.4m) long x ¾in (19mm) diameter

A number of rods for the weave: 8ft (2.4m) long x 1¼in (31mm) diameter (the higher the hurdle, the more weaving rods are needed)

Recommended tools

Billhook, brace and ⅝in (16mm) auger bit, loppers, draw knife, carpenter's square.

MEET THE MAKER

Darren Hammerton

I visited Darren Hammerton, a hurdle maker and woodland craft practitioner in his woodland 'Little Horsecroft Copse' in Hampshire in the south-east of England. It was a cold winter's day and Darren made a hurdle and shared his passion about managing his woodland and making craft produce. In particular, he expressed his love of making wattle hurdles from hazel.

"What I like about hazel is the products you can make from it, that's the attraction for me. If you're going to be producing hazel products commercially you need a lot of it. I normally need about an acre a year; that gives me about 800 to 1000 rods from an on-cycle coppice like Tegleys Copse, where I have been cutting this year. I don't just make hurdles, I supply stakes and binders for hedge laying and rods for other hurdle makers and people making continuous-weave fences. It was truly magical when I first cut some hazel up here, bearing in mind the hazel had not been cut since the 1960s. Georgie May, he's about 96 years old now, was the last person making hurdles here. Here's me 45 years on starting it all again."

There are different regional patterns of hurdles that occur in England. The regional differences are in the weave, and for this project Darren is making a garden wattle screen with a Hampshire pattern weave.

"You get a feeling like you are weaving the magic when you weave the wattle. The feel of the wood, the splitting of it, it rives really nicely; it's just lovely material to work with."

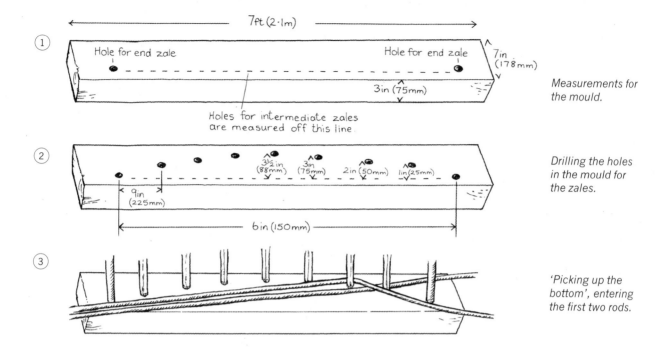

① 7ft (2·1m)

Hole for end zale   Hole for end zale   7in (178mm)

3in (75mm)

Holes for intermediate zales are measured off this line.

Measurements for the mould.

② 3½in (88mm) 3in (75mm) 2in (50mm) 1in (25mm)

9in (225mm)

6in (150mm)

Drilling the holes in the mould for the zales.

③

'Picking up the bottom', entering the first two rods.

Making the mould

To start the hurdle you need a mould. This can be a planked piece of wood or cleft out of a log. The mould must be heavy enough to hold the uprights (zales) steady as you weave the hurdle. When making hurdles in the woods, the mould is often pegged and tied down with a withe (twisted hazel rope). The holes in the mould are drilled out in a curve and angled so that the zales sit slightly backwards to ease weaving. The curve ensures that when the finished hurdle is released from the mould, it tightens and straightens as the cleft wood follows the curve. Hurdles are then usually stacked with some weight on them to encourage them to fully flatten.

Inserting the zales

Mark out the positions of the zales on the mould with a pencil and a carpenter's square ①, ②, drilling the holes right through it at a diameter of ⅝in (16mm). Choose two straight rods about 1¼in (31mm) diameter for the end zales. Point the thicker ends with a long taper and knock them firmly into the mould. The length of the zale will determine the height of the hurdle you are weaving. Cut the zales 6in (150mm) longer than the intended finished height for trimming up at the end.

Next, choose the intermediate zales. These should be straight rods of around 1½in (38mm) thick. Cleave them with a billhook (or other chosen method of cleaving) and use the pairs in matching positions within the curve of the mould. The first pair should go next to each end zale, working towards the middle. Darren recommends rounding the edges of the intermediate zales with a draw knife as this helps to stop the weave cracking. The cleaved face, with freshly exposed wood, should face into the curve in the mould.

Weaving in the base

Next it is time to 'pick up' the bottom of the hurdle. This weave is important to ensure the bottom of the hurdle stays together when it is taken out of the mould when finished. For this you will need six rods of about ¾in (19mm) diameter. Four of these should be 7ft (2.1m) long and two rods of 9ft (2.7m) long. When working this stage of the hurdle, work from the inside of the curve of the mould.

Take the two long rods and lay them as shown in picture ③. Leave about 3ft (90cm) beyond the end zale for twisting and tying in later. Make sure there are no knots in the rod just beyond the end zale as this is where the twist will occur. Next, place the other four rods into the mould ④. Each of these begins with its butt end against a zale and is woven in. The last two rods will form the tying-in rods to the left of the hurdle (looking at it from inside the curve). When weaving these rods, it is helpful to put your foot on the rods between the zales as you lift the rod and weave it behind the next zale.

④

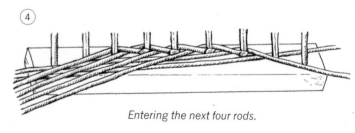

Entering the next four rods.

⑤

Twisting the hazel, strong wrists are helpful.

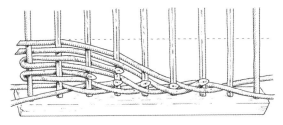

⑥ *Weaving the base.*

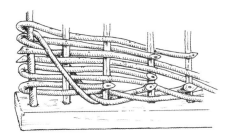

⑦ *Tucking in the tying-in rods to complete the base.*

Once you reach the end zale, take the rod back around it – this is where the twisting of the fibres occurs ⑤. Hold the rod firmly near the end zale and begin to bend it, at the same time twisting the rod through 360 degrees. Work the rod back and forth to loosen the fibres, but ultimately it is one strong twist (strong wrists are helpful) and the rod will turn back on itself and you can start to weave back the other way.

Continue with the other rods until your hurdle resembles ⑥. Next are the tying-in rods to complete the base. They are brought up, one on each side of the hurdle, and tied in place ⑦.

The cleft weavers

Now it is time to add the weave and raise up the height of the hurdle ⑧. For this you will need riven (split) rods of about 8ft (2.4m) in length. Having riven the rods with a billhook ⑨, they should be woven into the hurdle in pairs. Weave in two from one end, then two from the other ensuring that the butt ends are inserted first. Always ensure the riven side of the rod (the flat side) faces into the curve. These cleft weavers must not be thicker than the zales and the thickest of them are best used near the base of the hurdle. When twisting cleft (split) rods, the twist should only be 180 degrees and not 360 degrees, which you need for the round rods.

Look out for any major knots in the rod. A knot that is twisted or put under pressure by weaving it against a zale will crack and break. Other important considerations are not to end two weavers on the same zale above one another, always trim back to the previous zale. Always start a new weaver on the same side of the zale, where the previous one has been trimmed off. Shorter sections can be used to fill in where necessary ⑩.

⑧

The base of the hurdle, all tied in and ready to weave.

⑨

Riving hazel with a billhook.

⑩

The mid-section woven with pairs of riven hazel rods.

(11) *Inserting the spur to secure the top.*

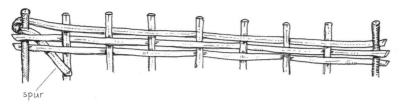

spur

(12) *The first top weaver woven in.*

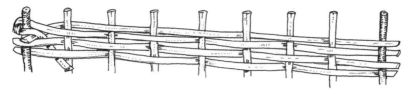

(13) *Second and third weavers of the top binding in place.*

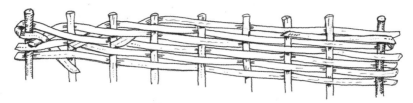

(14) *Double twist around the end zale.*

(15) *Finishing the top with the two round rods.*

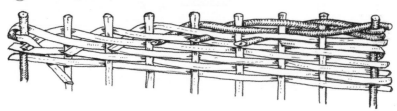

Weaving in the top

The top of the hurdle is tied in with a pattern to make it secure in a similar way to the bottom of the hurdle. Aim to finish the riven weave at the right-hand side (looking at the cleft face of the hurdle from within the curve of the mould), about 3in (75mm) lower than the left. You will then need four further cleft weavers about 8ft (2.4m) in length and two round rods of a similar thickness to the rods at the bottom of the hurdle. One will need to be 4ft (1.2m) and the other 8ft (2.4m) in length.

Take the butt end of the first weaver and then force it downwards at an angle of about 45 degrees into the weave so that it emerges about four rows down and appears in front of the zale. This angled end of the weaver is known as the spur. Twist it around the end zale and then weave it along the hurdle ⑪. Insert the next weaver beneath the twist and under the spur against the end zale and weave along the hurdle ⑫.

Next, tuck the butt end of the next riven weaver beneath the previous two you have woven, angled down so that the butt ends rests against the first intermediate zale from the left (looking at the cleft side of the hurdle). Weave it into the hurdle. Take the last riven weaver and follow the same procedure as the previous one, just tucking the butt end behind the second intermediate zale from the left ⑬.

Take the shorter of the two round rods and tuck it under the top two rows of weave at a similar angle to the last two riven weavers, so that it sits against the cleft face of the third intermediate zale from the left (looking at the cleft face of the hurdle). Weave this rod along the hurdle but do not take it behind the round end zale for now, leave it sticking out. Insert the longer of the two round rods under the top two rows of weave at a similar angle so that it sits against the cleft face of the middle zale. Weave the rod along the top and then create a double twist around the round end zale ⑭. Weave back along the top of the hurdle, tucking the end of the rod under the weave at an angle so that it appears in front of the fifth intermediate zale from the left, looking at the cleft face of the hurdle. Pick up the end of the shorter two round rods, bring it over the top of the weave and tuck it behind the end round zale, so it sits on top of the double twist ⑮.

Finishing off the hurdle

Trim up the hurdle, cutting off any weavers that stick out beyond a zale and trim back the top of the zales to an even height. Traditionally this would be done with a billhook or axe but the invention of strong loppers makes this part of the job easier and gives a tidy finish.

A finished wattle hurdle.

Tips for hurdle making

Keep checking that your zales are staying upright. Use measuring rods to check the width and height of the hurdle periodically. This will help achieve an even hurdle. If you are working on a frosty morning, warm the rods before weaving as they will twist and bend more easily and are less likely to crack. Many hurdle makers have a sheet of corrugated iron over a fire warming their rods during the cold of winter.

Using a peeling jig amidst freshly felled sweet chestnut coppice.

WOVEN PANEL

The woven panel makes a good alternative to hurdles if the twisting of fibres is too much for your wrists, you have poor-quality hazel, different species available or they just seem too complex. I have been making these, either as individual panels or for large areas of fencing, for a number of years. I have made them using hazel that is too poor to twist and from young sweet chestnut that does not twist and return on itself. In fact, any material can be used provided it is supple enough to weave. Think about the durability of the material and whether to use cleft older rods or younger rods in the round.

Materials you will need

1 plank: 6in (150mm) wide x 2in (50mm) thick (the length of this plank will determine the width of the woven panel)
2 upright frame poles: 4ft 6in (1.37m) long x 4in (100mm) diameter (this length will give you a 4ft (1.2m)-high panel – choose longer poles if you want a taller panel)
1 pole to be cleaved for the top and bottom rail: 4ft (1.2m) long x 4in (100mm) diameter (choose a longer pole if you want to make a wider panel)
48 cleft rods for weaving: 4ft 6in (1.37m) long x 1¼in (31mm) diameter (this is enough for a 4ft/1.2m-high panel – allow 12 cleft rods per 1ft/30cm of height)
5 poles for the zales (uprights): 4ft 6in (1.37m) long x 1¼in (31mm) diameter

Recommended tools

Cordless drill, 1in (25mm) auger bit, ⁵/₃₂in (4mm) drill bit, 4in (100mm) nails, 2½in (63mm) nails, 1in (25mm) chisel, maul, froe, cleaving brake, cleaving adze, billhook, loppers, bow saw, side axe.

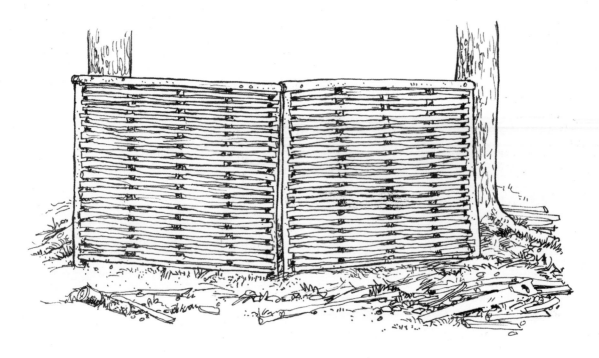

Cleaving chestnut using a froe.

The tongue ready to insert into the slot.

The tongue inserted.

The assembled frame.

Making the frame

Use a plank as a temporary support to keep the posts upright by screwing the posts to the end grain of the plank. The length of the plank will determine the width of the hurdle. In this example the plank is 4ft (1.2m). Cleave the top and bottom rail into two pieces using a froe and cleaving brake ⓵. Pilot drill the top rail and then nail it (using the 4in/100mm nails) into the top (end grain) of the posts, ensuring the distance between the posts once it is fixed on is 4ft (1.2m).

Insert the bottom rail into the posts by creating a tongue on each end of the rail and a chiselled slot in the posts. I use a 1in (25mm) chisel and lay it over the end grain of the cleft bottom rail and then mark each edge of the chisel with a pencil, so that two parallel lines 1in (25mm) apart are clearly visible on the end grain of the cleft rail. Use the same chisel to mark two parallel lines on the post. Saw the lines on the post with a bow saw and then chisel out to leave a slot. Offer the lines on the end grain of the cleft rail up to the slot to determine the length of the tongue. Once decided, make cuts with the bow saw at a right angle to the pencil lines and then use the chisel to take out the waste and leave the tongue ⓶. Pilot drill the tongues and skew nail them to the posts ⓷, ⓸. Skew nailing means driving in the nails at an angle rather than straight, to avoid them pulling out. Two nails are often used at opposing angles. Be careful not to cut too deep into the posts when making the slot as this could weaken the panel.

Drilling out holes for the zales using a cordless drill and a 1in (25mm) bit.

Hole drilled for a zale in the bottom rail.

The weave on its way up.

Inserting the zales

Fix the two end zales by pilot drilling and then nailing to the centre of the posts using the 2½in (62.5mm) nails. The number of zales inserted to weave around will depend upon the length of the panel and the flexibility of the weaving material used. In this project I am putting in three intermediate zales and the holes for them will be 1ft (30cm) apart. I use a 1in (25mm) auger bit. I drill the holes into the top and bottom rails about 1in (25mm) deep ⑤, ⑥. The zales can be shaved down at the ends with a side axe to approximately 1in (25mm) or else a rounding plane can be used for an exact fit. The zales are then inserted into the hole in the bottom rail and bent so that they fit into the top hole. If the zale has been cut to the correct length, any bending should have straightened out.

Weaving the panel

Now begin the weave. Take your cleft rods and weave in and out of the zales, trimming any surplus that overlaps the end zale with loppers. Alternate the weave each time as this will tension the rods against the zales. Leave yourself a few thinner rods for the top of the panel as these are the hardest to weave in ⑦, ⑧, ⑨.

The panel three-quarters finished.

A completed woven panel.

Assembling the panels

When constructing a long line of panels for use as a garden fence, it is easier to dig the posts into the ground (use a durable species) and then fix the top rail halfway across the top of the post, so that the panels link up as one continuous fence (10). It is also possible to vary the weave and put in extra rails to create a panel of your choice (11).

Panels with posts dug into the ground, forming a continuous fence. The posts and the cleft rods are all sweet chestnut.

Panels made with an extra rail and a criss-cross pattern top. The frames and rails are peeled sweet chestnut, the cleft rods are hazel.

Sweeping the deck with a besom broom.

BESOM BROOM

The main craft use of the birch tree comes from its twigs rather than timber – for the making of brooms. The besom broom is very practical but the user needs a little education. Modern-day brooms with upright handles have removed the understanding of how to sweep with a besom. Used correctly, with the broom outstretched and a sideways sweep, it is more effective than many of the modern alternatives. I use a besom for sweeping the decks around my house but it is also very effective for workshops and gardens.

Materials you will need

Twigs for the brush: 2–3ft (60–90cm long)
1 pole for the handle: 4ft (1.2m) long x 1¹/₂in (38mm) diameter
Galvanized wire, or traditional materials: (see box on page 57), for binding
Small piece of ash: for the peg

Sourcing the materials

As with so many woodland crafts, the term 'using what you have got' is a good place to start but if you can find young birch (about 6–10 years old) with thick crowns (cut in winter) they will make the ideal material for a besom. The handle needs to be about 1¹/₂in (38mm) diameter and about 4ft (1.2m) long. I have used chestnut as that is what I have readily available but you could also use ash.

Recommended tools

Billhook, side axe, wire cutters, pliers, besom grip, loppers, draw knife, whittling knife.

① 10in (25cm) Diameter

Traditional double binding on a 10in (25cm)-diameter broom, a triple binding would be used on a 12in (30cm)-diameter broom.

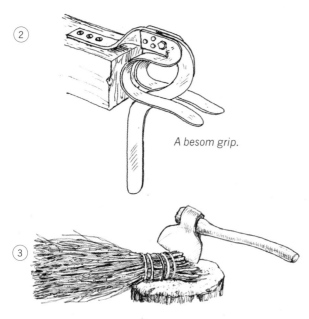

② *A besom grip.*

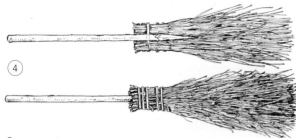

③ *Trimming the besom head with an axe.*

Making the head

Take a bundle of seasoning birch twigs and sort through them. Put taller twigs into one stack for the centre of the broom and the shorter twigs into another stack for the outside of the broom. Gather the taller twigs together to form a bundle. If you are wearing a leather apron, you can roll them on the apron to form a tighter bundle. Then arrange the shorter sticks around the core of tall sticks. The finished besom head will usually be 10–12in (25–30cm) diameter.

Binding the broom

This can either be done with traditional binding (see box opposite) ① or with galvanized wire. To help the binding process the twigs can be clamped tight in a besom grip ②. This enables the twigs to be compressed tight while the maker binds the head. Once the grip is released the twigs expand against the binding and further tighten the besom head. If you are using galvanized wire, pliers are used to twist the wire to tighten it further. Once bound, place the besom on a chopping block and use a small axe to trim the ends evenly ③.

Fitting the handle

Peel the handle with a draw knife and form a tapered point on one end to help it enter the head more easily. Make a blunt point on the other end to stop the handle splitting when it is impacted hard against a chopping block to help push the handle in firmly. The handle further tightens the bindings as it is forced into the head. Whittle a peg about 3in (75mm) long and about ¹/₂in (12mm) wide and then insert it through the head and into the handle, to keep it in place. A nail will also suffice. Finish by trimming off any stray twigs with loppers or a billhook ④.

④ *Cross section showing fitted handle and peg (the bottom one is the finished broom).*

A selection of finished besom brooms.

TRADITIONAL BESOM BROOM MAKERS

The traditional besom maker in Sussex was known as a broomsquire. A broomsquire would bundle and stack birch twigs and protect them from the weather so that he had stock for the coming year. Heather was also harvested for its bushy stems that were gathered from the heaths and commons during March. Stems would be 2–3ft (60–90cm) long and would be bundled and stored like the birch twigs. Handles were harvested from the coppice with ash and hazel commonly used. Traditional besoms were bound using fresh strips of binding material that varied depending upon what was available locally. It could be strips of ash, hazel or chestnut, pulverized bramble, willow or lime bast.

SPLIT-HANDLE
HAY RAKE

Wooden rakes used for traditional country tasks such as haymaking looked set to disappear in the British Isles, but with the resurgence of low-impact farming and, in particular, the scything of grass, traditional ash rakes are making a come back. Handcrafted wooden rakes are light, well balanced and an item of beauty as well as a practical tool.

TYPES OF RAKE

The two main types of hay rakes are the bowstay rake, formed with a bow of hazel to support the rake head (northern in origin) or the split-handle type found in the south. Larger drag rakes were used in fields without rocks and bumps where the extra width was useful without increasing effort.

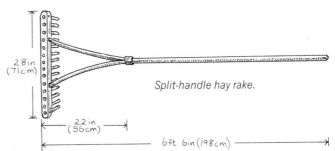

Split-handle hay rake.

28in (71cm)

22in (56cm)

6ft 6in (198cm)

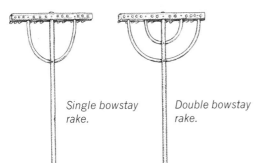

Single bowstay rake.

Double bowstay rake.

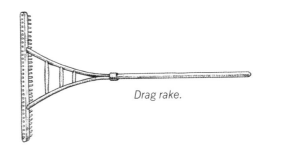

Drag rake.

Materials you will need

1 pole for the stail: 6ft 6in (198cm) long x 1¹/₂in (38mm) diameter
1 pole for the head: 28in (71cm) long x 4in (100mm) diameter (enough for two heads)
1 ash log for the tines: 1ft (30cm) long x 1ft (30cm) diameter
Tin plate or thick wire: for securing the split
Nails: 1in (25mm) and 1¹/₂in (38mm)

Recommended tools

Stail engine, draw knife, froe, Japanese ripsaw, side axe, tine cutter, maul, tin snips, hammer, knife, brace or cordless drill, calipers, selection of auger bits.

FEATURES OF A RAKE

The size of a rake is chosen depending upon the type of grass to be raked and the height of the user. Having a well-balanced, light rake is essential, especially if you are to be raking all, or most of, the day. Another important factor is the smoothness of the stail (handle). The stail must slide easily through the hand as it is drawn back and forth during the raking process. Although a rough pair of working hands will smooth it with continued use, ensuring a smooth stail to begin with is better. A stail engine is used to do this – an adaption of a rounding or rotary plane with a block of wood clamped to it. An adjustment on the block by loosening the screws creates a smooth taper along the stail. The head is also usually made from ash and is cleft. Holes are then bored for the tines (the prongs that stick out of the head), which are again made from ash.

A stail engine.

Cleaving the stail with a froe.   *The finished split stail.*

Splitting tine blanks from an ash log with a froe and maul.

A tine-making bench – the finished tines should collect in the bucket below the tine cutter.

Finished split-stail hay rake (centre) and two bowstay rakes either side.

Making the split stail

The size of the rake can be adapted for the purpose of its intended use. See drawing (previous page) for the measurements used in this project. Choose a six-month seasoned ash pole for the stail of about 1½in (38mm) diameter and remove the bark using a draw knife. Next, set the stail engine (see box on previous page) to smooth the stail and create a gentle taper.

Cleave the stail using a lath froe (or use a Japanese ripsaw) down the pole for approximately 24in (60cm) (1). Prior to cleaving, the split must be secured with thick wire or tin plate where it the split is to stop and meet the fully round part of the stail. This will prevent the stail from being split completely in two and will stop it opening any further (2). The split ends that go into the head can be further shaped to about ½in (12mm) diameter with a draw knife or rounding plane.

Making the tines

The tines are cleft to ensure that they are strong. Take an ash log of about 12in (30cm) diameter and cross cut it into rounds 5½in (140mm) in length. Mark a grid on the top with a pencil and cleave out the tine blanks using a froe and maul (3). Hammer the tine blanks through a tine cutter to produce the finished tines (4). These should be about ½in (12mm) in diameter. Leave the finished tines to season for a month or more or dry them out in a greenhouse or near a stove for a couple of weeks.

The head

Cleave the rake head from a round of about 4in (100mm) diameter and shape with a side axe and draw knife to create a lightweight head. This head should be made with greenwood to help it shrink tight onto the handle and tines. The head should finish with dimensions of approximately 28in (71cm) long x 1½ x 1½in (38 x 38mm).

Assembling the rake

Drill two holes for the split stail to attach to the head. Check the diameter of the split stail with calipers and then choose the appropriate drill bit. A nail is hammered through the head to secure each split half of the stail. Some rake users prefer a slight angle for the stail from the head so the angle of drilling should reflect this. Mark and then drill holes into the head for the tines. The shrunken diameter of the tines can be checked with calipers to ensure the right-sized holes are drilled. The head, being green, will shrink and the tines will be gripped tightly, so no other fixings are necessary. The tines should be lightly sharpened with a knife to finish.

CHESTNUT
PALING FENCING

One of the wonderful characteristics of sweet chestnut is its ability to split easily, making it popular for craft use. Chestnut pales are the cleft pieces from round logs. These pales can be used for a number of purposes but it is when they are bound together with twisted galvanized wire that they form the familiar rolls of chestnut paling fencing. These rolls of pales are ideal for temporary as well as permanent fencing as they can easily be rolled up and transported to another place and used again. During the Second World War, rolls of pales were used as temporary roads as they could be unrolled across difficult terrain to help provide access.

Materials you will need
Sweet chestnut poles: lengths vary from 3–6ft (90–180cm) (see page 63). They should be 3–6in (75–150mm) in diameter
Galvanized wire: to connect the pales
Staples: for attaching the paling fence to the fence posts

Recommended tools
Bow saw, froe, cleaving brake, maul, draw knife, hammer, staple gun, fencing tighteners

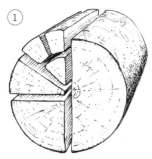

Breaking the round down into pale sections.

Detail of cleaving the pales with a froe.

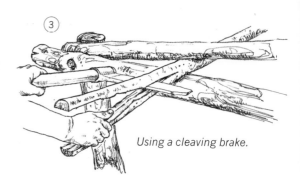

Using a cleaving brake.

Splitting pales on a cleaving brake at Prickly Nut Wood.

Making the pales

Pales can be made from rounds of wood of 3in (75mm) to 6in (150mm) in diameter. Peel the bark off using a draw knife and then split the round in half using a froe and then into quarters and so on (1), (2). A froe is commonly used in conjunction with a cleaving brake (see page 202) (3), (4) to give more control of the cleaving process. The cleaving brake allows the craftsman the opportunity to realign the direction of the split during the cleaving process (5). A 6in (150mm) round can make 24 pales (6). The wood you use needs to be reasonably straight grained, but the quality does not have to be as good as the chestnut chosen for lath making.

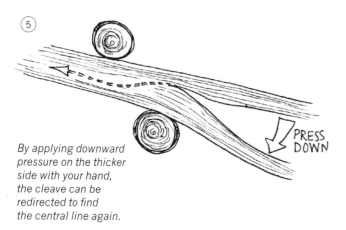

By applying downward pressure on the thicker side with your hand, the cleave can be redirected to find the central line again.

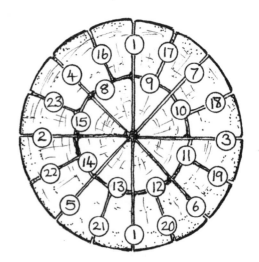

(6) 24 pales can be cleft from one round. The first cleave cuts the log in half, shown by two number 1 labels.

Bundles of 25 pales ready to be processed into paling fence.

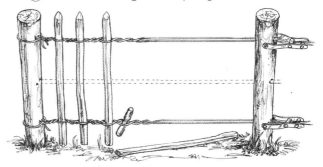
8 Device for making chestnut paling fence in the woods.

Pales are made in lengths from 3–6ft (90–180cm) high. Standard sizes include 3ft 6in (105cm) and 4ft 6in (137cm). Occasionally there is demand for 2ft (60cm)-high pales, mainly for decorative fencing. When making 6ft (180cm)-high pales, the best wood is used but if the cleave runs out then you may still get a 4ft (120cm) pale from it. Once cleft, the pales are finished with a blunt point at the top and then bundled tightly to ensure they do not warp or bend before being made into chestnut paling fencing (7).

Making the fencing
Secure two posts into the ground (these are part of the tightening device) with fencing tighteners attached at one end. The wires are fed through and the pales inserted. The wire is twisted between each pale by using a wooden peg like a Spanish windlass (8).

Erecting the fence
Install the paling fence by driving chestnut stakes into the ground. Fix the fence to them either by drilling through a pale and nailing to the fence post or stapling the wire to the fence post. Rolls can be easily joined together to get a long continuous length. Although pales are thin pieces of wood, they last a very long time as a fence as they are not buried in the ground (9) and are made from the heartwood of durable sweet chestnut.

The pales sit on top of the ground and therefore last a long time.

Completed 6ft (1.8m) rolls in the foreground with bundles of pales waiting to be made into rolls of fencing behind.

Chestnut pales being inserted and twisted on the bed.

The reels of wire that feed the bed for making paling fence.

THE MECHANIZED SYSTEM

Although the method described on page 63 is used by some coppice workers in the woods for making paling fence, most supply bundles of pales to a local fencing manufacturer who has a mechanized system for wiring the fence together. I dropped in on J.E. Homewood and Sons of Haslemere, Surrey, who began making paling fencing in 1946 and continue to this day. Steve Homewood, who runs the company, has been a helpful source of employment and information to many who work the woods in the local area.

The manufacturing process consists of a long bed with reels of wire mounted at one end. The wires feed into a twisting head, which does the job of the Spanish windlass in seconds. One person feeds the pales in between the wires and a roll of either 16½ft (5m) or 33ft (10m) is completed. The wires are then stapled to every pale alternating top and bottom. The shorter rolls are for the larger pales to make them a manageable weight to move.

A wired roll of fence is stapled before being rolled and removed from the bed.

POST-AND-RAIL
FENCING

Post-and-rail fencing is usually made from sweet chestnut or oak. There are many variations but the fence usually comprises two or three rails that have been cleft and are then tenoned rustically before being slotted into mortises in the posts. The posts, if they are sawn, are usually oak or chestnut, or occasionally a durable softwood like European larch. If they are cleft or in the round, they will be sweet chestnut, although oak posts can be used if they are shaped to remove the sapwood.

Materials you will need
Chestnut pole: 10ft (3m) long x 1ft (30cm) diameter (will make four rails)
Chestnut pole: 6ft (1.8m) long x 10in (25cm) diameter (will make two posts)

Recommended tools
Wedges, side axe, chainsaw, carving bar, chain mortiser, brace and bit, bar auger, corner chisel, lump hammer, cleaving brake, froe.

Cleaving the chestnut post with axe head and wedges.

Two cleft chestnut posts.

A selection of cleft chestnut rails.

Preparing chestnut cleft post and rails

The posts will vary in length depending on the particular fence. I look for chestnut rounds of between 10–12in (25–30cm) diameter and these are then cleaved using wedges. Find the centre of the log and hammer in an axe head to open up the cleave. As the cleave opens, insert a wedge into it and continue hammering to open it more (1). Continue this process until the log splits in two (2). It is best to find a straight-grained log, but if a knot is on one side it is possible to cleave out two posts, provided the cleave does not pass through the centre of the knot.

For cleaving the rails I look for an approximately 10ft (3m) length of 12–14in (30–35cm)-diameter chestnut. This can be slightly curved, as part of the character of this fencing is the unevenness of the rails. In order for the fence to look good, rails should be paired up as they are split, so that the curves in each bay follow the same lines. Cleave the rails out in the same way as the posts but, once halved, each piece is cleaved again to form four rails from each length of timber (3). If you are having difficulty with run-off while cleaving the rails, they can be inserted into a cleaving brake (see page 202) and the cleave can be controlled with a heavy froe and the brake.

Making the tenons

The rails are then 'ended' by creating a rustic tenon. This can be done by using a chainsaw or side axe, or a combination of both (4). The key is to make sure the tenoned ends line up and are in the same plane (5). After the first tenon is cut, position the rail so that the first tenon is vertical before cutting the other end. Large-scale producers take the rails back to a workshop and cut out the tenons on a band saw.

A chainsawed tenon can be smoothed off with a side axe or rasp.

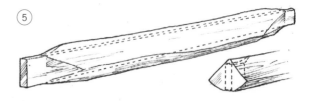

Ensuring the tenons are in the same plane.

Chainsawing a mortise using a carving bar.

Chainsawing a mortise. Two parallel cuts are made and then a gently curving cut on each side to meet the first cut.

Making the mortises

The distance between mortise heights in the post will depend upon the particular style of fence (see box overleaf), but I find 20in (51cm) from the centre of one mortise to another gives a well-balanced look. The mortises can be made in three ways. The first and most rustic is to use a chainsaw. Care needs to be taken when plunging to keep the depth accurate. A carving bar attached to the chain saw will improve accuracy ⑥, ⑦. The second is to use a chain mortiser ⑧. This clamps onto the post and produces a very clean and accurate mortise. Clamping it onto cleft posts as opposed to sawn takes practice and a wedge may need to be added to the vice part of the mortiser if the cleft post is a bit wobbly. The third is to drill the mortise with a bar auger ⑨ or brace and bit and then clean out the holes using a chisel. A corner chisel can be useful for ensuring the corners keep a right angle ⑩.

Erecting the fence

Put out a string line to ensure the fence is straight (provided that is the objective). Dig a hole about 2ft (60cm) deep and tamp the first post firmly in position. Dig the second hole a rail's distance from the first. Put the second post in the hole but do not backfill or tamp. Slide the rails into the mortises of the first post and then bring the second post up to a vertical position sliding the tenons of the rails into the mortise. This is best done with two people, especially if it is a triple-rail fence. Then back fill and tamp. Continue this process by digging the next hole a 'rail's' distance from the second post. At the end check all rails are firm. If any are loose, hammer a 'key' into the mortise ⑪. 'Keys' are made from the offcuts when cutting out the tenons on the ends of the rails.

Using a chain mortiser to cut a mortise.

Drilling out a mortise using a bar auger.

Using a corner chisel to ensure right-angled corners.

Using 'keys' to secure the rails.

Variations of style

A post-and-rail fence using sweet chestnut posts and rails.

A variation of post-and-rail fencing with added cleft palisade.

A post-and-rail deer fence 6ft 6in (198cm) tall. This pattern of added pales has been shown to deter deer from jumping the fence.

LOCAL VARIATIONS

In Sussex this type of fencing is a vernacular style. There are even variations in how the posts are mortised from East to West Sussex. The mortises in the West Sussex style are usually 3in (75mm) deep by 1¹/₂in (38mm) wide, whereas the East Sussex double mortises are usually 3in (75mm) deep by ³/₄in (19mm) wide. With the West Sussex style, 'keys' (a wooden wedge) are hammered into the mortise to firm up the rails if there is any movement of the rails in the mortise.

ABOVE: The double-mortise style of East Sussex and single-mortise style of West Sussex.

A post-and-rail field fence where the rails form a diamond pattern to protect trees planted along the fence line. Note the Sussex 'Oigg' (capping) on top of the chestnut gate post.

DIAMOND
TRELLIS

There are a wide range of patterns that can be used to make trellis panels. They can be delicate, with small rods from hazel or willow, or larger and more durable ones made from timbers like sweet chestnut. This Diamond Trellis falls into the latter category. It is a pattern I have returned to many times as it makes an aesthetically pleasing trellis, which is relatively easy to construct.

Materials you will need
Roundwood poles to make one panel
2 poles for the end posts: 8ft 6in (2.6m) long x 4in (100mm) diameter
2 poles for the top and bottom rails: 6ft (1.8m) long x 4in (100mm) diameter
4 poles for the central diamonds: 3ft (90cm) long x 3¹/₂in (88mm) diameter
4 poles for the inner diagonals: 2ft 6in (76cm) x 3¹/₂in (88mm) diameter
4 poles for the supports: 1ft (30cm) x 3¹/₂in (88mm) diameter

Recommended tools
Bow saw, chisels: 1in (25mm) and 2in (50mm), carpenter's square, tape measure, boat level, hammer and nails, cordless drill, impact driver and timber locks, portable vice (superjaws) or carpenter's trestles and ratchet straps.

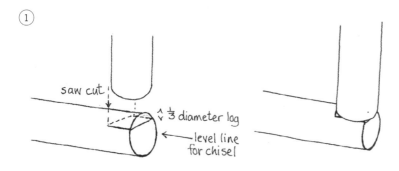

Marking the poles for constructing the corner joint.

The finished joint at the corner of the diamond.

The completed square that will become the diamond.

The 45-degree cut into the end grain that supports the central diamond.

The finished support fits to the central diamond.

Top and bottom rails

The top and bottom rails of the trellis are constructed in the same way as the rails in the woven panel project. See page 51 for instructions.

Making the central diamonds

The diamonds are actually a square, which is then turned to become a diamond shape. Take four 3ft (90cm) poles and make sure the end cuts are all straight. Secure one pole in the vice or ratchet to the carpenter's trestles and, using the boat level, mark a line about one third of the way down the end grain. Measure the diameter of the piece of wood that will fit to the one you have marked and measure back from the end grain

that distance. Saw down to the depth of the level line you have marked (1). Using a chisel, cut out from the level line to the saw cut. Fit the second pole into the joint then drill and nail them together (2). Continue for all four poles and you will have created the square that becomes the central diamond shape (3).

Supports for the central diamond

Make up the four supports for the central diamond by making two cuts at approximately 45 degrees to the sawn end grain at one end of each pole (4). This creates a right angle into which the diamond will sit (5).

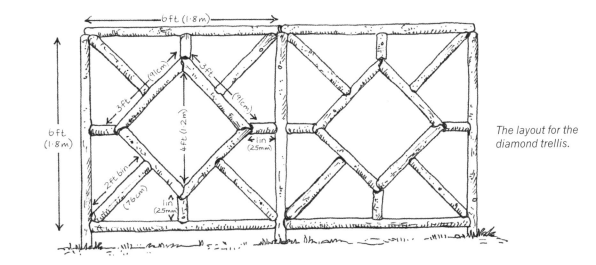

6

6ft (1·8m)

6ft (1·8m)

3ft (91cm)

3ft

(91cm)

4ft (1·2m)

1in (25mm)

2ft 6in (76cm)

1in (25mm)

The layout for the diamond trellis.

The completed panels.

Assembling the panel

These panels can be constructed in the workshop but are easiest to build in their final location as the end posts can be sunk into the ground. If you are constructing a row of panels, mark out the position of the end posts with a string line and dig the holes so that they are sunk 2ft (60cm) into the ground.

Fit the panel together following the layout (6). Fix the bottom support to the centre of the lower rail. This needs to be pre-drilled and fixed. Nails can be used, but timber locks ensure a solid fixing. Next, position the diamond in the bottom support while fitting the top support to hold it in place (an extra person helps here). Secure the two side supports and the diamond will be secured in place. Finally, shape the ends of the four diagonals to fit snugly into the corners of the panel and secure to the midpoints of the diamond. A number of these connected together make a striking trellis in the garden.

GATE HURDLE

The traditional use for gate hurdles was for 'folding' sheep. Although not commonly used in this way any more, like the wattle version they are finding their way into gardens as fencing and plant supports. One of the strengths of the gate hurdle is the rounded oval mortise and tenon: this ensures the rails do not twist yet it is relatively quick to make.

Materials you will need
Roundwood poles for one hurdle – these are actual sizes so allow a little extra
1 pole for the heads: 4ft (1.2m) long x 3¹/₂in (88mm) diameter
3 poles for the rails: 6ft (1.8m) long x 3in (75mm) diameter
1 pole for the braces: 5ft (1.5m) long x 3in (75mm) diameter
1 pole for the strop: 3ft (90cm) long x 3in (75mm) diameter

Recommended tools
Bow saw, froe, cleaving brake, draw knife, shaving horse, side axe, drill and auger bits, template gauge, twybil, hammer, nails.

FOLDING SHEEP WITH GATE HURDLES

Where I live on the edge of the South Downs in West Sussex, sheep were traditionally folded as they grazed. Folding involved keeping the sheep in a particular strip and, once grazed, they were folded onto the next strip. This way, the sheep were kept in one area and the risk of worm infections was far less. The fencing used to keep them in was the gate hurdle. They were often fixed together with a metal ring permanently attached around the head between the top and second rail. This ring would loop over the top of the next hurdle and the heads were tapped, sinking the hurdle 6in (150mm) into the ground. Stability was achieved in the zigzag pattern of the hurdles.

Gate hurdles being used to fold sheep on the South Downs.

Pointing the base of the heads.

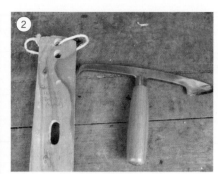

Template gauge and twybil.

Shaping the rounded tenon at the end of a rail with a draw knife.

Using the template gauge to check the size of the tenon.

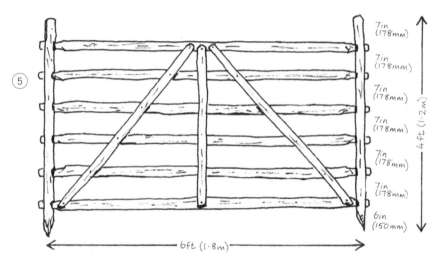

Layout and dimensions for a gate hurdle.

Preparing the timber

Select straight timber for the head and rails. The braces can look good with a curve. The best timbers are sweet chestnut and ash but any local timber that cleaves well and lasts a few years would be suitable. Split the head, rails, braces and strop in two using the cleaving break (see page 202) and a froe. You will have a spare strop, so pick the best. Take the heads and, using a side axe, make a point at the base ends of both heads ①.

Forming the tenons

Using the shaving horse and draw knife, peel the half-round rails and round off the edges. Using the template gauge, form rounded tenons on each end of the rails ②, ③, ④.

Laying out the hurdle

I use my workshop floor and lay out the heads at right angles to a good level floorboard 6ft (1.8m) apart. Lay the heads cleft side up so that the rails can be laid over them and the position of the mortises can be marked. The rails should be laid out at 7in (178mm) centres, the first being 6in (150mm) from the bottom of the heads ⑤.

Marking the rails where they cross the heads, to show top and bottom of the mortise position.

Using the template gauge to draw the mortise positions.

Drilling out two holes for the start of the mortise.

Using the twybil to cut between the drilled holes to form the mortise.

Using the 'ferret' end of the twybil to remove the cut wood.

Fitting the rail tenons through the mortises.

Nailing through the mortise and tenon joints.

Completed chestnut gate hurdle.

Making the mortises

Mark both sides of each rail where they cross the head ⑥. Remove the rails and position the template gauge centrally on the head between the two lines you have drawn. Now draw round the inside of the template to mark the mortise positions ⑦. The template gauge I used is 1½in (38mm) long x ⅝in (16mm) diameter. You can make smaller or larger templates depending on the size of material you are using to make the hurdle. Next, drill two holes in each mortise with the drill and auger ⑧. For this project I used a ⅝in (16mm) auger. The surplus wood between the holes is removed with a twybil (mortising knife). This is a lovely tool and has been designed perfectly for this particular job. The blade is used as a knife to cut between the drilled holes ⑨ and the curved end (ferret) is used to remove the cut wood ⑩.

Assembling the hurdle

Insert the rails through the rounded mortises in the heads ⑪. Once they are all in place, square up the hurdle by laying it out on the workshop floor again. Check the dimensions and that the diagonal measurements across the hurdle are equal. Then pre-drill and fix them with nails ⑫. I recommend ring shank nails for strength. If they are not available, use longer nails and clench (hammer flat) the ends where they come through to the other side of the hurdle. Now, with the hurdle laying with the cleft faces of the rail towards you, fix braces and the central strop. Again pre-drill and nail to complete the gate hurdle ⑬.

WOOD FUEL

Logs

Sourcing quality firewood, 'reading' a log to know how to split it, and seasoning and preparing kindling are all part of a woodsman's craft. Prior to the arrival of coal in the 17th century, wood was the staple fuel across the British Isles. Woodlands were shaped and managed by the need to cut and process firewood for warmth and cooking. Across the wooded pastures of Britain, trees were pollarded and the resulting branches gathered for firewood. Pollarding ensured that the regrowth sprouted above the height of grazing animals. Such management systems developed in order to achieve a sustainable supply of wood fuel.

WOOD-FUEL BOILERS

With coal diminishing and the need for renewable energy on the rise, wood fuel has again increased in importance in the British Isles with improved wood-fuel boilers and government incentives to set up such systems. Most of these systems involve the slow feed of boilers with wood pellets or chips, although there are now a number of log batch boilers available. As a woodsman, it is these that I recommend, as the others are reliant on the extra process of chipping or forming pellets. If the chipper breaks down or the pellet delivery doesn't arrive, you cannot use the boiler. With a log batch boiler, if your log splitter breaks down you can always pick up an axe and keep the boiler fed, warming yourself through the age-old meditative process that is log splitting.

Felling trees

Felling trees must be done at the appropriate time. The best time for this will be during the winter, when the sap is down and the wood will have less sap in it and will dry out more quickly. Felling trees is a dangerous activity and it is important to be properly trained. This training varies from country to country, but in Britain, if you are felling trees for work, you need to be assessed and pass the relevant units by an instructor with NPTC (National Proficiency Training Council) approval. The industry standard qualification is essential if you are working in woods and even for hobby users this course is highly recommended as it will teach you good maintenance and safe use of the chainsaw. Cross-cut saws and axes can also be used but careful felling and attention to detail of the cuts you make are essential if you are to become proficient and safe at felling trees with hand tools.

Seasoning and stacking

Once felled, the timber then needs to be stacked where it will get a good breeze blowing through it, for example, on the edge of the wood facing the prevailing wind and not under the canopy of other trees.

If the wood is a large diameter, splitting it down with wedges will make it lighter to extract and speed up the seasoning process. Seasoning is the process of reducing the moisture content of the wood and will begin from the moment the tree is felled. If the tree is still standing, it will start to season if it has been ring-barked or has died.

The best way to dry wood is to split it to its finished size and stack it so it can air-dry in an open-sided barn on pallets, or a raised slated floor to help with airflow. This is the ideal, but most of us do not have a barn and, if we do, drying firewood may not be the best use of its space. Stacking on the edge of a wood with a good airflow and possibly a sheet or two of corrugated steel or 'onduline' (corrugated sheets of plant fibre and bitumen) laid over the top will be a good starting point for seasoning the wood. I try to avoid using tarpaulins as the wood can sweat beneath them and condensation can form on the inside, resulting in poor drying conditions for the wood.

Mixed firewood of ash, birch, alder and hazel are seasoned for a year; beech and hornbeam for 18 months, oak for two to three years and sweet chestnut preferably three years (see table on page 81). One of the advantages of seasoning sweet chestnut at the edge of the wood is its natural durability. Many other woods would be deteriorating and rotting after three years but chestnut will be fine for many years and this is a great help when you have a limited covered area for storage.

A woodland firewood stack.

Chestnut logs seasoning with a good airflow on the edge of the wood.

Stages for felling an upright tree.

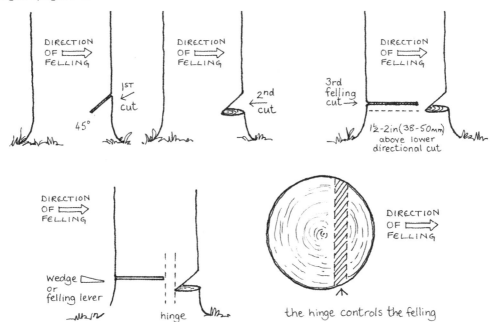

DIRECTION OF FELLING

1ST cut

45°

DIRECTION OF FELLING

2nd cut

DIRECTION OF FELLING

3rd felling cut →

1½-2in (38-50mm) above lower directional cut

DIRECTION OF FELLING

Wedge or felling lever

hinge

DIRECTION OF FELLING

the hinge controls the felling

Safe escape routes when tree felling.

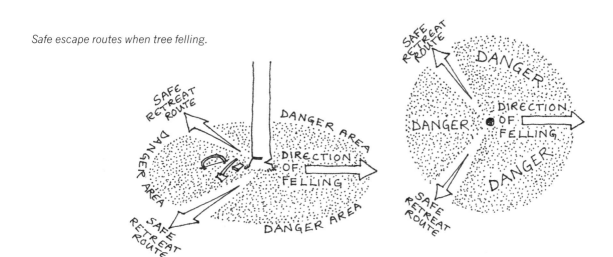

SAFE RETREAT ROUTE

DANGER AREA

DANGER AREA

DIRECTION OF FELLING

SAFE RETREAT ROUTE

DANGER AREA

SAFE RETREAT ROUTE

DANGER

DANGER

DIRECTION OF FELLING

DANGER

SAFE RETREAT ROUTE

Seven splits are made for eight logs.

A chopping block with a back to prevent split logs from falling off.

Inverting the axe and using the weight of the log.

Splitting logs

Wood can be split with a log processor, hydraulic log splitter or by hand. Splitting wood by hand with a good-quality splitting axe is a timeless pleasure. I have lived on no other fuel but wood for the past 23 years, splitting every log with an axe. Each year I gain more pleasure from this seasonal task and the satisfying feeling as the shed fills up with winter fuel all gathered in.

The old saying, 'it warms you twice', is true enough; after ten minutes of splitting logs you will be shedding a layer of clothing. I use a splitting axe as opposed to a splitting maul as I find them heavy and cumbersome. Splitting mauls rely on weight and brute force to gain access with the large wedge-shaped head whereas a splitting axe is lighter, more precise where it strikes the log and the wedges on each side help open the log with each swing. As with all tools it is a personal choice but if you choose a tool that suits you, chopping firewood becomes a craft of reading each log.

Large logs need to be split by taking the edges off first; I use a seven-split system to produce eight logs. If the axe gets stuck in a log try inverting it and using the weight of the log to help. There is a range of specialist wedges available for splitting awkward logs, which can be useful, but I prefer to chainsaw knotty logs into large lumps I call 'keepers'. These I use last thing at night to ensure my fire has stayed in until the morning. The more knotty the piece of wood, the longer it will take to burn.

I have two compartments in my log shed. I fill both sides before each winter and as one is used up, it is refilled with extracted seasoned logs as I use the other. This alternating process ensures I always have a good supply of dry firewood for myself and to supply locally.

The head of a splitting axe.

The head of a splitting maul.

Rumford fireplace at Prickly Nut Wood.

THE AVERAGE SPEED OF DRYING LOGS

I took a 6–8in (150–200mm) diameter round log and then split it in half and then again into quarters. The table reflects the increased speed of drying for the logs that were split. The logs were stored with weather protection.

Species	Drying time for 6–8in (150–200mm) diameter log	Drying time for cleft log (split in half)	Drying time for quartered log	Comments
Ash	1 year	9 months	6 months	Will burn green
Alder	1 year	6 months	3 months	Burns fast
Apple	2 years	18 months	1 year	Scented
Beech	2 years	18 months	15 months	
Birch	1 year	9 months	6 months	Burns bright, bark good firelighter
Cherry	2 years	18 months	1 year	Scented
Chestnut (sweet)	3 years	2 years	18 months	Spits
Hawthorn	2 years	18 months	1 year	
Hazel	18 months	15 months	1 year	
Holly	2 years	18 months	1 year	
Hornbeam	18 months	15 months	1 year	
Larch	2 years	18 months	1 year	Spits
Oak	3 years	2 years	18 months	Burns slowly
Sycamore	18 months	15 months	1 year	
Willow	1 year	9 months	6 months	Burns fast
Yew	3 years	2 years	18 months	Burns slowly

The log sheds at Prickly Nut Wood.

Bags of logs at Prickly Nut Wood ready to supply the village shop.

Firewood split, stacked and drying thoroughly in a log shed.

LOGS TO BURN

There are many versions of this old rhyme.
This one comes from Edlin's *Woodland Crafts in Britain*.

Logs to burn! Logs to burn!
Logs to save the coal a turn!
Here's a word to make you wise
When you hear the woodsman's cries

Beech wood fires burn bright and clear
Hornbeam blazes too,
If the logs are kept a year
To season through and through

Oak logs will warm you well
If they're old and dry
Larch logs of pinewood smell
But the sparks will fly

Pine is good, and so is yew
For warmth through wintry days
But poplar and willow too
Take long to dry or blaze

Birch logs will burn too fast
Alder scarce at all.
Chestnut logs are good to last
If cut in the fall

Holly logs will burn like wax –
You should burn them green
Elm logs like smoldering flax
No flame is seen

Pear logs and apple logs
They will scent your room
Cherry logs across the dogs
Smell like flowers in bloom

But ash logs, all smooth and grey
Burn them green or old,
Buy up all that come your way
They're worth their weight in gold

Anon

Kindling

A steady supply of dry kindling is as essential as the seasoning of your logs. Good fire craft involves the gradual building up of a fire, starting with tinder, moving on to kindling and then on to fire wood.

ABOVE: Collecting kindling from an eight-year-old sweet-chestnut coppice. As the coppice grows, some of the smaller stems are shaded out creating easy-to-collect dry kindling.

Sources of kindling

One advantage of kindling is that it can be collected and dried out quickly. If you work or have access to a wood, it is not difficult to pick up a bag or box of kindling from twigs on the ground. If you are fortunate enough, like myself, to work in a coppice woodland there will always be dead shoots and side branches to collect that have been air dried as they are still standing. If you make craft produce and use a shaving horse, you will also generate a steady supply of quality kindling. 'Brashings', the dead side branches pruned from coniferous plantations, make an excellent kindling.

Commercial kindling is usually made up of softwood and can, with the aid of a kindling processor, be a good way of utilizing poor-quality plantation material or thinnings. I have sold bundles of rhododendron kindling that, when seasoned, are excellent for starting fires.

PIMP MAKING

For the ultimate kindling I have to turn to Alan Waters who has revised the work of Mr. Greenfield, a pimp maker from Plaistow in West Sussex, during the 1950s. The pimp is a circular 'wheel' of kindling and consists of 25 individually tied small bundles of birch twigs with cleft hazel. These are placed in a circular iron frame and cut to length with a billhook. The frame acts as the mould for the final 'wheel' of kindling. The pimp is then tied with a natural cord like hemp or sizal before being removed from the mould. These pimps then make an attractive and functional kindling craft to light up any fireplace.

The iron frame of a pimp being filled with individual bundles of kindling.

A completed pimp.

FAGGOTS

Faggots are made from the 'lop and top', the brash from cut coppice stems. These twiggy ends were traditionally bound up and used to fire bread ovens. The faggot burnt away inside the oven and, once it had heated it and finished burning, the ashes were scraped out and the bread put in. Other uses have been for civil engineering works where the faggot forms a drain below the ground so water can pass through it. Faggots are now most commonly used for river revetment work where they help reduce erosion and benefit soil stabilization. I have made faggots from sweet chestnut in large quantities for the Environment Agency. This is only possible when I am cutting sweet chestnut on a short rotation and, even then, the brash is not so well feathered and easy to fold in as that from hazel.

(1) *A faggot jig.*

(2) *Rough dimensions of a faggot.*

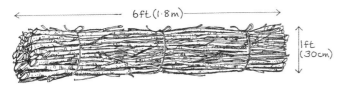

6ft (1.8m)

1ft (.30cm)

Two finished faggots.

Materials you will need

4 poles for the cradle: 3ft (90cm) long x 2in (50mm) diameter
1 forked pole: 3ft (90cm) long x 2in (50mm) diameter
1 pole for the handle: 1ft (30cm) long x 1½in (38mm) diameter
Brash: up to 6ft (1.8m) long
Steel cable: 8ft (2.4m) of 5/16in (8mm) diameter
Bailer twine: for tying the finished faggot
Wooden toggle: for securing the steel cable

Recommended tools

Billhook, loppers, chainsaw (for cutting finished faggots
to length), jig, measuring stick.

Making the jig

Drive two pairs of 2in (50mm)-diameter stakes into the
ground at opposing angles of about 45 degrees. Tie them
where they cross over at about 6–8in (150–200mm) above
ground level, forming a raised cradle for the brash. The two
pairs should be in line about 5ft (1.5m) apart. A forked stick
(prog) should be driven into the ground centrally between
the two pairs at 45 degrees with the forked end pointing
downwards. Drill the stick just above the fork, pass a 5/16in
(8mm) steel cable through the hole and wrap it around a
wooden toggle to stop it pulling back through the hole.
About 8ft (2.4m) of cable is needed. At the other end of
the cable loop it around the handle and secure (1).

Filling the cradle

Sort through the brash and begin to lay lengths into the
V-shaped cradle. It is preferable to use lengths that span
the whole length of the finished faggot, which is 6ft (1.8m),
but shorter lengths can be used up in the middle. The finished
faggot should have a diameter of about 1ft (30cm). Once the
cradle is full, pass the steel cable underneath the faggot and
then wrap it around twice, pulling on the handle to tighten up
the brash as you go. The handle is then locked off, by passing
it back through the fork of the inverted prog. With the cable
holding the brash tight, the faggot can be tied off centrally and
at each end with bailer twine. The raised cradle makes it easier
to pass the twine under the brash.

Use a billhook to trim off any twigs sticking out and then
lay a 6ft (1.8m) measuring stick beneath the faggot and saw
the ends off to the exact measurement while it is still in the
jig. Release the steel cable and the faggot can be removed from
the jig (2). **Caution:** Be careful when tying the central cord of
twine not to tie the steel cable into the faggot!

CHARCOAL BURNING

Charcoal burning must surely be one of the oldest crafts associated with the woods. Pollen analysis from 5,000 years ago shows up charcoal deposits being present. The production of charcoal by burning wood with a restricted air supply preceded the first smelting of metals to make tools. Charcoal was the only available fuel for smelting metal through the Bronze and Iron ages. Charcoal is still used by some traditional tool-making blacksmiths but most use coke in their forges. The main uses today for charcoal are for barbecues, artist's charcoal and bio-char, a charcoal dust added to the garden as a soil sweetener.

TRADITIONAL CHARCOAL BURNING

Traditional burns were carried out in pits and, later, above ground in earth-covered kilns. The charcoal burner and family would live in the woods, tending their kilns. As fire broke out through the turf layer, the charcoal burner, constantly vigilant, would shovel more earth over the turf and restrict the flame from igniting. In Britain, earth burns are now only carried out by charcoal burners to keep the tradition going and are usually seen as a woodsmen's social event!

A traditional charcoal-burner's hut.

THE EXETER RETORT

Nowadays, most charcoal burning in the woods is carried out in portable steel-ring kilns, although the trailer-mounted 'Exeter retort' is trying to establish its cleaner, more efficient burning system as a preferable alternative. Retort kilns produce less pollutants and re-burn the gases usually emitted from a ring kiln, ensuring a higher proportion of charcoal is produced in a shorter period of time.

To make charcoal in a
RING KILN

I have been making charcoal for 23 years in a ring kiln and produce predominantly barbecue charcoal and some artist's charcoal from peeled sticks of willow, oak, chestnut and spindle. I also produce bio-char by crushing the charcoal fines, which are a by-product of every burn.

Ring kilns come in a variety of shapes and sizes. Some are two rings high, and 8ft (2.4m) in diameter. I have two 6ft (1.8m)-diameter single-ring kilns. I like this size as it is a good single-person kiln. It is easy to unload and bag up the kiln, clean it out, refill it and light it in a day if you are working on your own.

Materials you will need
Seasoned logs: approximately 1 ton (1,016kg)
Kindling
Soil or sand
Chicken-wire frame: for riddling the charcoal (see page 94)
Wooden chocks: to support the lid
Peeled sticks of willow, oak, chestnut and spindle: for the artist's charcoal
Old biscuit tin and sawdust: for packing the artist's charcoal
Steel cable

Recommended tools
Kiln, shovel, gauntlets, large crow bar, chainsaw, sharp knife, splitting axe, head torch, drill, protective clothes and mask.

Choosing where to site the kiln
It is important to site the kiln very carefully. Charcoal kilns produce a vast amount of smoke and a poorly placed kiln can upset close neighbours. One charcoal burner I know caused the M25 motorway in the south of England to come to a standstill until the kiln was put out! Think about the prevailing wind direction and where the smoke is likely to drift. I light my kiln in the evening so that the main smoke production is emitted during the night. Try to burn on a calm, still night as the smoke will rise vertically rather than drift and you will have a more successful burn.

The hearth is the name of the area where the kiln will be sited. Try and find a level site. If this is not possible (which is often the case in the woods), you will need to dig out a flat hearth into the hillside or slope and dig a drainage channel to shed water away from where the fire will burn.

Drying out the hearth
A 6ft (1.8m)-diameter kiln has six vents (metal feet) that it sits on, a larger kiln usually has eight. These vents are spaced evenly around the circumference of the kiln, and the kiln is placed on top of them. Although a ring kiln is a heavy item, they are relatively easy to move in the woods as they can be turned on their side and rolled like a large metal wheel.

With the kiln positioned on top of the vents, burn a small bonfire inside it, without the lid on, to help dry out the hearth. The hearth will be cold to begin with and this fire will dry out the ground first to make the charcoal-making process more successful. The more successional burns carried out on the same hearth, the drier the hearth becomes and the faster and more successful are the results of each charcoal burn.

Loading the kiln
The following day after the bonfire on the hearth, it is time to load the kiln. In order to have some control over the fire during the burn, it is essential to keep the channels from the vents clear to the centre of the kiln. This is done by placing logs in a cartwheel pattern towards the centre, making sure that the logs are placed each side of the vents and have a good clear channel to the centre of the kiln. Place the next layer of logs over the top of the cartwheel, following the circular pattern of the kiln ①. This ensures that the air channels are kept clear in the early stages of the burn. Fill the centre of the kiln with kindling and place any 'brown ends' (not fully converted logs from a previous burn) on top ②. Then fill the kiln with logs, following the circular shape and packing them in as tightly as possible. In the 6ft (1.8m) ring kiln, I try to use 4in (100mm)-diameter logs in the round. If the logs are larger, I split them in half. If they are smaller, I place them to the outer edges and near the top of the kiln.

① *Laying out the bottom of the kiln. Air must have a clear channel from the vent through to the centre of the fire.*

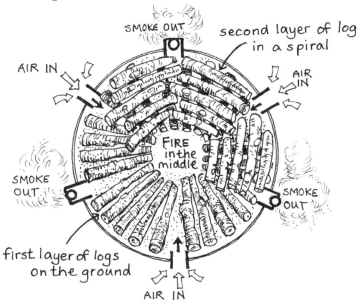

SMOKE OUT

second layer of log in a spiral

AIR IN

AIR IN

SMOKE OUT

FIRE in the middle

SMOKE OUT

first layer of logs on the ground

AIR IN

② *Charcoal burning using a ring kiln.*

stack smaller bits right up to here (it will shrink)

wood chocks to let the smoke out at first

six or eight air vents

put the brown ends near the middle

kindling

larger wood towards the bottom of the kiln

AIRFLOW IN
The kiln sits on metal feet

AIRFLOW OUT
The chimney sits on the feet

THE FIRE IS LIT through a port with paraffin on a rag tied to a stick

Once the kiln is nearly full, add sticks of willow for making artist's charcoal if you want to make it in the same burn. Cut the sticks to about 8in (200mm) in length and carefully peel the bark from them using a sharp knife. At this stage they look like a greenwood pencil. I collect old biscuit tins (there are usually plenty of them being recycled after Christmas!). Pack as many sticks as you can into the tin ③ and then tightly fill it with sawdust. The sawdust fills in the gaps and stops the sticks bending in the heat of conversion to charcoal. Drill the lid to make a few small air holes and then tie it on with steel cable. Position each biscuit tin between the chimneys, near the top of the kiln ④.

Continue to fill the kiln and then place three wooden chocks to support the lid during the freeburn part of the process. Make sure you have plenty of soil or sand available, ready to shovel onto and around the kiln as the burning gets underway. A good pair of gauntlets is essential as you will be moving hot chimneys midway through the burn, a head torch (if you are burning at night) and you will need to make sure the access around the kiln is clear of obstacles.

The burning process

I light my kilns by pushing a stick with a lighted paraffin-soaked rag through an air vent towards the kindling in the centre of the kiln. I do this through at least two vents. Some burners still use a central stick when they are packing the kiln. They then pull out the stick, and pour hot embers into the centre of the kiln. This process involves lying across the timber in the kiln and adding the lid once the fire is burning. Lighting through a vent with the lid chocked up is a safer method.

As the kindling ignites the fire begins to burn and smoke swirls out from under the lid as if it is a burning cauldron. The fire will crackle and pop and the intensity of smoke will increase, this is the freeburn part of the process ⑤. Air is able to enter the kiln from all around the circumference and exit all around the circumference under the chocked-up lid. As the fire burns it will spread out to the edge of the kiln; this may take an hour or more if the hearth is freshly made, but once the hearth has been baked after a few burns, it should only take 30 to 40 minutes. Once embers are dropping between the logs at the edge of the kiln, it is time to earth up between the vents ⑥, ⑦.

Peeled sticks in a tin, ready to be made into artist's charcoal.

Positioning the tin for artist's charcoal between the chimneys, near the top of the kiln.

The early part of the burn is the part that produces the most smoke.

Once embers are clearly dropping at the edge of the kiln, it is time to earth up between the vents.

Earthing up between the vents.

Blocking off the draw through the vent.

Encouraging draw through the vent.

Gases burning off.

Looking through the air vent.

This will be a gradual process to begin with and, after you earth up one, it will speed up the process as the fire is pushed out towards the edge between the next two vents. As you are earthing up, you can position the chimneys on alternate vents and block off the draw through the vent to the fire (8). On the vents that are to be kept open, the draw can be encouraged by blocking off the top of the vent where the chimney attaches (9).

Once the chimneys are in place it is time to remove the chocks and drop the lid. This is a dramatic moment in the burn as the change of draw when closing the lid often results in the ignition of gases around the base of the kiln (10) and sometimes around the lid. Often flames will burn out through the air vents, so it is important not to be standing in front of one of them when you drop the lid. Once the lid is down, it is time to shovel earth around the lid edges to create a seal. At this point the freeburn is over and the kiln is under control.

The chimneys will now be drawing and after another 30 minutes, the fire should have settled down. There should be a strong draw of smoke through each chimney and when you look through the air vents the fire should be glowing orange (11).

The kiln will continue to burn like this with a restricted oxygen supply until it is ready to close down. I usually swap the chimneys and vents over midway through the burn to help even out the burning process. With a 6ft (1.8m) kiln this will be about five hours after lighting. Wearing gauntlets, lift each chimney off its vent and move it to the adjacent vent that had previously been drawing air in. Repeat the process to block off the draw and encourage the draw, shown in pictures (8) and (9).

TYPES OF WOOD FOR CHARCOAL MAKING

I only use seasoned wood for making charcoal and if you follow the table I have used for drying logs (see page 81), the wood should be perfectly seasoned for charcoal conversion. Both hardwood and softwood can be used for making charcoal. Hardwood is preferable for barbecues as it burns hotter and breaks down less in the kiln, but if your main interest is bio-char then softwoods are a good choice. The best woods for making charcoal are alder and hornbeam followed closely by beech. Oak and chestnut make a good charcoal as does overstood hazel or birch.

Metallic blue smoke shows it's time to close down the kiln.

Opening the kiln.

Opening the biscuit tin of artist's charcoal.

Riddling and bagging up – protective clothes and masks must be worn.

Local charcoal, straight from the woods.

After 11–13 hours, depending on weather conditions and how well-baked the hearth was before lighting, the chimneys will have reduced to producing a small amount of transparent smoke with a metallic-blue sheen to it (12). This is the time to shut down the kiln. Remove all the chimneys and use earth to block off all inlets into the kiln.

The kiln now needs to be left to cool down. If you open it too early, oxygen may re-ignite the charcoal. I leave my kiln to cool for 48 hours, which is longer than necessary but ensures that it is fully out. Opening the kiln is always an exciting moment as it reveals how well the burn has gone (13), (14).

Processing the charcoal

The charcoal from the kiln needs to be riddled. Protective clothes and a mask must be worn for this. Sieve out the small charcoal fines through a chicken-wire mesh frame. The large lumps of charcoal stay on top and the small pieces fall through the mesh (15). With a 6ft (1.8m) kiln, I average around 265–309lb (120–140kg) per burn and this is then bagged up and sold through local outlets (16). The charcoal fines are then rolled and made into bio-char (see box below).

BIO-CHAR

This is crushed charcoal made from wood or plant material and is in demand for gardens and vegetable production. It is almost pure carbon and chemically inert. It improves soils for growing as the bio-char retains moisture and nutrients and helps plants to mycorrhizae (a symbiotic relationship between fungi and plant roots) as the roots penetrate the cavities in the bio-char.

Bio-char made from rolled or crushed charcoal fines being used on the vegetable garden at Prickly Nut Wood.

To make charcoal in a
45-GALLON DRUM

This is a small-scale method of making charcoal, which should appeal to anyone who wishes to make their own barbecue charcoal, forge their own tools or make bio-char for their garden using waste wood.

Materials you will need
45-gallon (205 litre) drum
Bricks
Kindling
Seasoned logs: enough to fill a 45-gallon (205 litre) drum
Tarpaulin
Wooden chock

Recommended tools
Angle grinder, lump hammer, drill, protective clothing and mask.

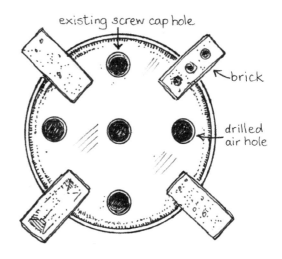

The holes and brick positions for the bottom of the drum kiln.

Cut the base out of the drum with an angle grinder about 1in (25mm) from the edge to form a circular lid. Using a lump hammer, shape the cut edge to form a lip upon which the cut-out lid will sit. Remove the screw cap from the top of the drum and drill four more holes of approximately 2in (50mm) diameter, as shown top right. Place the drum on four level bricks.

Begin a fire in the bottom of the drum with a good amount of kindling and get it burning well. Begin to add seasoned wood of 3–4in (75–100mm) diameter and add this randomly to the fire. As the fire grows stronger, speed up the process of adding wood. Larger pieces can be split down in size. Once the kiln (drum) is full of wood and is burning well, earth up around the base leaving a single channel into the underside of the kiln. The lid can now be placed on top but with a wooden chock to hold it open and allow smoke to exit at one side. This smoke will be thick and white. Knock the side of the drum with a piece of wood as the burn progresses to encourage settlement and get all of the wood to the heart of the fire.

After about three hours the white smoke will have reduced and the smoke will become clear with a metallic-blue sheen. This is the time to shut the kiln (drum) down. Earth up the final channel at the base of the kiln and pull out the chock and let the lid down. Earth over the lid to create a seal. When you are confident that no smoke is escaping, the kiln must be left to cool for at least 12 hours. The final stage is to remove the earth from the lid and open the top of the kiln. The kiln can then be tipped over onto a tarpaulin and, wearing protective clothing and a mask, the resulting charcoal sorted and bagged.

The different stages of burning charcoal in a 45-gallon drum.

CRAFTS FOR
BUILDING

LATHS

Cleft laths, made primarily of sweet chestnut but occasionally of oak, have a growing market in the UK. Traditional timber-framed buildings with lime plaster use laths as they provide a better surface for the plaster to adhere to. Eco-builders are utilizing more lath as they favour the use of natural, breathable plasters like lime and clay as opposed to cement-based ones.

Materials you will need
Sweet chestnut poles (known as blanks when making laths):
4ft (1.2m) long x ideally 3–8in (75–200mm) diameter but can be larger.

Recommended tools
Triangulated cleaving brake, draw knife, froe, billhook, peeling jig.

Meet the Maker

Justin Owen

I went to visit Justin Owen and family who work chestnut woods for the National Trust in Haslemere, Surrey. Justin and his family make 30,000 linear ft (9,144m) of lath every month. Justin began as a yard boy for a local paling firm and took every opportunity that came up to get out into the woods. The business is a family affair, with sons Jack and Curtis now working along side him, Justin has the next generation not only learning the crafts but, in the case of Jack at age 22, creating the laths faster than Justin can. Seventy percent of their business comes from making laths. The rest is made up of fencing, oak pegs and a little charcoal. They are restoring a valley of chestnut coppice that Justin remembers walking through with his grandfather the last time it was cut. For me, it is a pleasure to walk through a valley and see the chestnut coppice being cut again and see the production of the laths in the woods.

"From the moment I went to help load pales onto a lorry, I knew I wanted to be in the woods. It's about reading the wood – you should be able to see what's in the tree before you fell it. Don't try to turn something into laths that isn't laths! I don't like to admit it but the youngsters can outdo me now."

Justin Owen cleaving laths in the chestnut copse.

Lath blanks ready for peeling.

Using a draw knife to remove the bark.

The blank cleft into segments ready to be further cleft into laths. Notice the straight grain: only the best wood should be selected for blanks.

Choosing and preparing the blanks

To make laths, the first thing to do is choose the right blanks to work from. These need to be as straight as possible, free of knots or with very minimal small knots and of a diameter between 4–18in (10–46cm) ①. The larger blanks will produce more and there is less peeling overall but they are heavier to lift and rotate. Place the blanks in the peeling jig and then remove the bark with a draw knife ②. Justin has a mechanical peeler but prefers to peel by hand.

Splitting the blanks

Split the blanks radially into halves, quarters, eighths and so on using a froe ③. Some lath makers work with smaller 3in (75mm)-diameter blanks and split them through and through rather than radially but, like Justin, I have always chosen to split them radially. Perhaps it is because I made pales before I made laths or that by making them radially, mixed-diameter sizes can be used.

Split the cleft segments down further using a froe and a triangulated cleaving brake (see page 202) ④.The cleaving brake gives the lath maker control over the cleave as the wood is split apart. If the cleave starts to run off, downward pressure on the thicker part will bring it back to the centre ⑤. The froe is a tool used for splitting and levering and for most crafts does not need a very sharp edge. However, with the smaller froes Justin uses, a sharp edge is needed as they also double as a rustic chisel to shave off any inconsistencies once the lath has been split.

LATH SIZES

Laths are made in a range of widths between 1³/₁₆in (30mm) and 1³⁷/₆₄in (40mm) but an average of 1¹¹/₃₂in (34mm). The lengths vary but the most popular is 4ft (1.2m).

Cleaving the lath on the triangulated cleaving brake.

Putting downward pressure on the thicker part while in the cleaving brake to control the split.

Shaving down the sides of a split lath with a billhook.

Finishing off the laths

Once the laths are split out, dress them down with a billhook to clean up any sapwood or inconsistencies in width (6). Tightly bundle them into batches of 50 (200 linear ft of 4ft lath to the bundle) ready to be used in a building project (7).

Using the laths

I have used cleft chestnut laths on a number of buildings. There are two techniques I use. One is to nail the laths with copper clouts to the studwork and then apply lime plaster over them (8). The laths should be dampened before applying lime and the gaps between them should allow for the lime plaster to pass between as well as covering them. The other method is to use zales and weave the laths around them (9). This is a useful technique when using earth plasters.

The finished laths piling up ready for bundling.

Chestnut laths being applied to a stud wall of the Lodsworth Larder – a community village shop built by the Roundwood Timber Framing Company.

Tip
for using laths

Time spent constructing a good cleaving brake (see page 202) that is set up at the right height for the lath maker will aid productivity and reduce back pain.

Woven chestnut lath with zales and earth plaster being applied.

SHINGLES AND SHAKES

Wooden roofing tiles are known as shingles or shakes. Shingles tend to be sawn, whereas shakes are cleft by hand and have a more rustic appearance. The sawn shingle has the advantage of being quick to produce and uniform – therefore easy to fit on a roof. The shake is made individually by hand so takes longer to make and fit but leaves, I feel, a more attractive finish. There are two main styles of making shakes, radial shakes and bastard shakes. I shall cover both methods. Both involve cross cutting a timber butt to the length of shingle required.

ABOVE: Fitting sawn Sussex western red cedar shingles.

RIGHT: The uniform look and easy fitting of sawn shingles makes them useful for more complicated roofs like this roundhouse built by the Roundwood Timber Framing Company.

Fitting shingles and shakes

When fitting shingles and shakes it is important to have a three-shingle overlap. In other words, the shingle or shake that you are fitting should overlap the shingle or shake below it and the one below that. You should begin with a double row at the bottom and an extra baton here will help the bottom row to sit in place. Each row of shingles or shakes should be offset from the row below, so that the edge of one shingle or shake is not in line with the one below.

Types of timber to use

The best timbers are oak, sweet chestnut and western red cedar. These are durable timbers and can be cleft successfully. As these timbers contain tannic acid, it is important to use non-corrosive fixings such as copper, bronze or stainless steel. With oak and chestnut, shakes will need to be pre-drilled prior to fixing to avoid splitting. With western red cedar, when using thin silicon, bronze or stainless steel ring-shank shingle nails this is not necessary. Other timbers can be used for shakes or shingles provided they are straight grained (if you are going to make shakes) and durable. It is a lot of work to make non-durable shakes, only to see them rot after a few years.

Cleft chestnut shakes on the roof at Speckled Wood, built for the National Trust by the Roundwood Timber Framing Company.

SHAKE SIZE

I make shakes 1ft (30cm) long as it makes the arithmetic for laying out the batons simple and there is less chance of run-off while cleaving if the wood is not of great quality. The cross cutting needs to be accurate to ensure the shingles are of the same length and angled cuts will be highlighted when the shingles are fixed on the roof, a characteristic you may or may not like.

To make
RADIAL SHAKES

Materials you will need

Clean, knot-free logs: 18in (46cm) diameter or larger, usually oak or sweet chestnut

Recommended tools

Chainsaw, draw knife, wedges, froe, shaving horse, maul, shake brake.

Radial shakes are made of timber butts of a diameter of around 18in (46cm), but larger sizes can be used. Cross cut a round to 12in (30cm) in length then split it in half ①, quarters and then eighths using wedges ②. If the grain is true and straight it will be possible to split it down further with wedges before reverting to a shake brake (see page 202) and froe. Remove the sapwood (this will be the lighter coloured wood between the bast and the heartwood) from each radial segment with a froe ③, leaving a large radial 'piece of cake', which is then inserted into the brake. Applying pressure to the thicker side will help control the cleave and allow thin shakes to be made ④. These are finished with a draw knife on a shaving horse (see page 202) to clean them up and bevel the bottom edge ⑤.

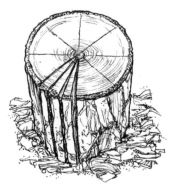

Radial shakes.

① *Beginning to split the oak round with wedges.*

② *The round split into segments.*

Removing the sapwood from a segment with a froe.

Cleaving the shake from the segment using a froe and for more control a shake brake.

The finished radial oak shake.

To make
BASTARD SHAKES

Materials you will need
Knot-free sweet chestnut logs:
approximately 8in (200mm) diameter,
or larger

Recommended tools
Chainsaw, froe, draw knife, side axe,
shaving horse, shake brake.

Bastard shakes.

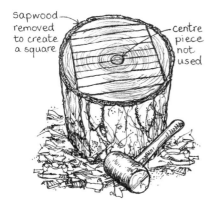

sapwood removed to create a square

centre piece not used

ADVANTAGES OF THE BASTARD SHAKE

Bastard shakes are the illegitimate version of the radial shake but have many advantages, the main one being they can be made out of small-diameter coppice wood. I make bastard shakes out of sweet chestnut, which, due to its very small amount of sapwood, means that 8in (200mm) rounds can be used. These are often achieved in a coppice system after 20–25 years of regrowth. From a productivity angle this is very important as an oak tree will often take 80 years to reach a desirable size for shake making, meaning that by using sweet chestnut you can increase productivity by at least two thirds.

Cross cut a round to 12in (30cm) in length then square it up by removing four slices of sapwood from the round (1). This leaves a roughly square block from which the shakes are cleaved 'through and through'. Use the shake brake (see page 202) as the block gets smaller (2). Discard the shake that runs through the centre of the round as it will split over time. Finish the shake on a shaving horse (see page 202) with a draw knife to bevel the end grain (3) and tidy up any unevenness on the sides with a side axe (4). These shakes will be useable for natural building but any knotted or uneven ones can be used for animal housing or play structures (5).

Removing the sapwood from chestnut segments.

Using the brake to cleave out the shakes.

Apprentices Paul and Millar finishing shakes with a draw knife at Prickly Nut Wood.

(4) *Finished shakes: the ones with knots will be used for animal housing.*

(5) *Chicken house at Prickly Nut Wood with chestnut shakes.*

Timber framing

To go into detail about the craft of timber framing is a separate book and has already been well covered, but to not include some of the basic joints and then look at the new vernacular of roundwood timber framing would be to miss out a key area of woodland crafts. The building of a house or barn hewn straight from a tree or constructed from round poles, felled and built within the woodland is the foundation of one's craft. Many woodland crafts have originated from the construction of timber buildings. For example, there is little point in making shakes or laths without a timber-framed building to utilize them.

An example of the English housing joint.

Styles of frame

In Britain, the earliest surviving timber-framed buildings date from the thirteenth century. Timber framing continued as a major building form in barns and houses until the early nineteenth century. Since then, timber-framed buildings suffered a decline in numbers until a recent revival where timber framing is once again being respected for the skill and interpretation of the craftsman. The choice of timber varied in these early buildings, often dictated by what was locally available and affordable but where it could be obtained, oak did (and still does) form the majority of timber-framed buildings in Britain. Timber framing styles and traditions vary across the globe with hubs of activity in America and Japan. In Britain, timber frames have evolved from the early cruck frames, where the cruck blades carry the roof load to the ground, to the box frame, where posts and wall plates carry roof trusses.

Joints used for cruck frames

The early cruck frames were formed by a pair of cruck blades, often cleft from one piece of wood to create a mirrored pair. These would rise from the ground and were joined by a tie beam to form an 'A' frame. On larger cruck frames a collar would also be used and the wall plates would sit on the extended tie beams. One key element of most cruck construction was the simplicity of the jointing where half lap joints were common, sometimes with a half dovetail in the collars to prevent spread of the cruck blades.

Joints used for box frames

In contrast to the simpler joints of cruck construction, the box frames that followed had far more complex joints, in particular the English housing joint. This joint removed the need for the curving presence of the cruck blades and created a larger open space in the building. The English housing joint consisted of a jowl post. In simple buildings this would be a post upturned so that the buttress flared out and could take the two tenons cut at right angles to each other. In more crafted buildings the jowl post would be hewn out of a larger round and the front taller tenon (known as the teazle tenon) would support the tie beam, which would then be dovetail lapped onto the wall plate located onto the rear tenon of the jowl post. The principal rafter would then be tenoned into the tie beam using a bridle joint or bird's-mouth tenon.

A cruck frame.

A box frame.

principal rafter →

tie beam

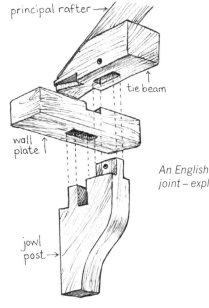

An English housing joint.

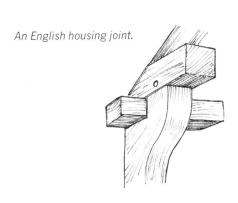

wall plate ↑

An English housing joint – exploded view.

jowl post →

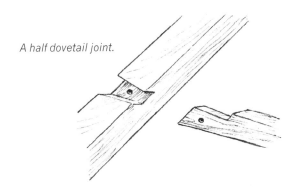

A half dovetail joint.

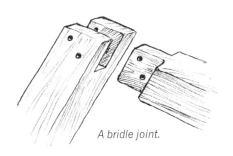

A bridle joint.

A simple scarf joint.

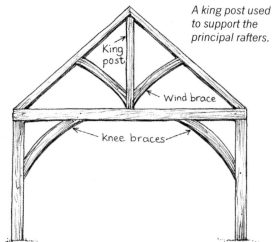

A king post used to support the principal rafters.

King post

Wind brace

knee braces

Length and width of timber frames

The length of a building was dictated by how many bents (frames) were constructed, and by the length of the wall plates. Where the wall plates were not long enough they were jointed together using a scarf joint. The variation and different styles of scarf joint are many – the one illustrated here is a simple scarf joint. The width of the building was dictated by the tie beams in each bent. To extend the span without using a middle supporting post, a king post was used in the centre of the tie beam to support the principal rafters. To increase the width further, a middle post was added to support the tie beam and two queen posts on top of the tie beam would support a collar tie attached to the principal rafters.

Other joints

Bracing is essential to avoiding racking or movement in a building and the lapped dovetail joint, which is let into the post, is commonly used to triangulate the frames. Other key joints are the dovetail, which can be useful for letting in joists after the main frames have been erected. The American housed dovetail is an improvement to the basic dovetail where larger joists are being let into the main timbers. One of the simplest framing joints is the mortise-and-tenon joint. This is used primarily to secure a post between the sill plate (running around the bottom of the building) and the wall plate above. A shouldered mortise-and-tenon is a useful adaption when fixing a horizontal beam into a vertical post.

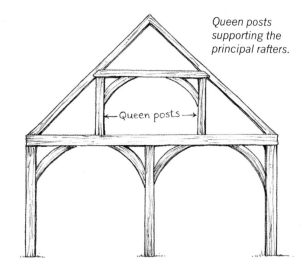

Queen posts supporting the principal rafters.

Queen posts

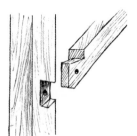

Lapped dovetail for knee braces.

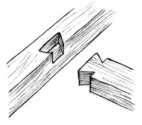

Dovetail joint.

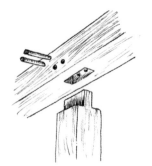

Mortise-and-tenon joint.

Shouldered mortise-and-tenon joint.

A roundwood timber-framed building made from European larch.

The woodland house 12 years after construction.

Roundwood timber framing

Early builders worked with wood in the round to construct their houses, barns and shelters. With the arrival of the saw mill and the relative ease of fitting together right-angled timber, the use of wood in the round faded into obscurity in developed countries. Traditional roundwood construction continued in areas where rural dwellings were needed. The ease of felling trees and then constructing in, or near, the forest outweighed the cost and effort of using sawn timber.

My interest in roundwood timber framing came from the desire to use the timber I had available in my wood. The majority of the wood is sweet chestnut (*Castanea sativa*), and is grown as a coppice system. Hence, I have a large number of reasonably straight poles of sweet chestnut, which are durable due to the small amount of sapwood and the high tannin content of the heartwood. They are too small in diameter to be milled, so when I came to build my house the obvious choice was to build in the round with sweet chestnut.

Many timber species are suitable for roundwood construction. I look for hardwood timbers that are durable and low in sapwood like sweet chestnut and black locust (*Robinia pseudoacacia*) and softwoods that are slow grown and reasonably durable like European larch (*Larix decidua*) and Douglas fir (*Pseudotsuga douglasii*). The other important considerations are the structural strength of the timber in bending and compression. I also have an unthinned European larch plantation and have been utilizing the slow-grown tall, thin poles to create a number of roundwood timber-framed buildings.

Over the last 12 years, I have worked on the development of roundwood timber-frame joints and, although there are a number of different options, it is the scribed butterpat joint that I use most commonly in roundwood construction. The following caravan project (see page 110) uses the butterpat and mortise-and-tenon joints. The frames constructed could also be put on padstones to make a small workshop or shed or scaled up to create much larger projects.

Roundwood timber-frame construction.

Reciprocal frame roofed roundhouse.

A sweet chestnut pole with clear definition of the darker heartwood and creamy-coloured sapwood of the outer circumference.

ROUNDWOOD TIMBER-FRAMED
CARAVAN

This project is to build an 18ft (5.48m) x 6ft 6in (1.98m) roundwood timber-frame caravan – a micro woodland home. The chassis has been welded out of channel steel and the axle and wheels are salvaged from an old four-wheel-drive vehicle. The details and measurements of the chassis are given in case you wish to weld one up to the exact dimensions. However, this design can easily be adapted to an existing chassis you may already have or can be placed directly onto padstones as a workshop. The basic steps for building the frame and cutting the joints can also be used in a similar way for building a larger frame for a house.

Materials you will need
Roundwood poles
Crucks: 4 at 12ft (3.6m) long x 7in (175mm) diameter
Posts: 8 at 8ft (2.4m) long x 7in (175mm) diameter
Tie beams: 4 at 7ft (2.1m) long x 7in (175mm) diameter
Ridge pole: 1 at 20ft (6.1m) long x 7in (175mm) diameter
Wall plates: 2 at 20ft (6.1m) long x 7in (175mm) diameter
Roof rafters: 10 at 6ft (1.8m) long x 5in (125mm) diameter
Front purlins: 6 at 5ft (1.5m) long x 3in (75mm) diameter
Rear purlins: 6 at 3ft (90cm) long x 3in (75mm) diameter
Zales: 8 at 2ft (60cm) long by 1¹/₂in (38mm) diameter
Split lath: 24 at 4ft (1.2m) long x 1¹/₂in (38mm) wide

Sawn wood
Underfloor beams: 4 at 7ft (2.1m) long x 6in (150mm) x 6in (150mm)
Floor joists: 8 at 12ft (3.6m) long x 6in (150mm) x 2in (50mm) (use initially for the framing bed)
Floor joists (including noggins): 12 at 7ft (2.1m) long x 6in (150mm) x 2in (50mm)
Roof rafters: 16 at 6ft (1.8m) long x 4in (100mm) x 2in (50mm)
Studwork (including noggins): 35 at 7ft (2.1m) long x 4in (100mm) x 2in (50mm)
Floorboards: 15 at 12ft (3.6m) long x 6in (150mm) x 1in (25mm)
Floorboards: 15 at 7ft (2.1m) long x 6in (150mm) x 1in (25mm)
Cladding (siding): 7ft (2.1m) high x 12ft (3.6m) length per side of caravan
Cladding (siding): 7ft (2.1m) high x 9ft (2.7m) length per end of caravan
Baton: approximately 250ft (76.2m) of 2in (50mm) x 1in (25mm)
The chassis: 4in (100mm) channel steel welded as in plan (see illustration below)

Recommended tools
Chainsaw, panel saw, de-barking spade, draw knife, chalk line, carpenter's square, spirit level, scribers, scribing pods, rounding plane, Japanese saw, hammer, maul, framing chisels, gouges, slick, drill, auger bits, fixings, ratchet straps.

A NOTE ON THE MATERIALS USED

I used waney-edged cladding, therefore extra was needed to overlap the boards. Depending on the size and design of the windows and door, the volume of cladding can be reduced to allow for these openings.

For the roof I used onduline sheeting made from organic plant fibre and bitumen as it is lightweight and copes with a low pitch and a moving caravan. If you wish to use shakes or shingles (see page 102) this can be done by increasing the roof pitch. Raise the position of the ridge when laying out and use longer crucks.

You will also need to decide what to use for the subfloor, internal walls and ceiling. They can be tongue-and-groove timber or sheeting. I used panelvent, a breathable particle board that is fixed together with natural resins rather than glue. I used 4in (100mm) of sheep's wool natural insulation in the walls, floor and roof. This makes a warm and well-insulated caravan. I finished the walls internally with clay paint, another breathable product.

I chose sweet chestnut for the crucks, posts, round roof rafters, zales and lath; European larch for the wall plates and ridge pole; Douglas fir for the underfloor supports, floor joists, roof rafters and studwork; and western red cedar for the floor and cladding. There are many other options available. I chose timbers that are suitable for purpose, durable and locally available in the woods.

Measurements for the chassis.

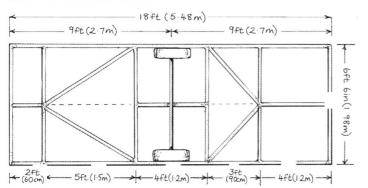

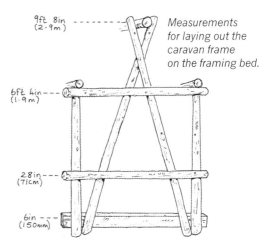

Measurements for laying out the caravan frame on the framing bed.

Peeling the poles using a draw knife.

Using a 3/4/5 triangle to check the framing bed is 'in square'.

Preparing the poles

The poles all need peeling. This can be done roughly with a de-barking spade and then finished with a draw knife to get clean, smooth poles for scribing ①.

Building the framing bed

The first step is to build a framing bed. The framing bed is a level horizontal platform upon which the frames are laid out for construction. If the framing bed is level, the frames will fit together well and, when raised, will stand vertical. The size in length and width of the framing bed will vary depending on the height and width of the frame you are constructing. I built these from 6in (150mm) x 2in (50mm) sawn timber, which can then be reused as the floor joists in the caravan or building. Screw together the sawn timbers for strength (remember they will need to be unscrewed later to be reused) and fix onto wooden posts that have been sunk into the ground. Add a second layer fixed at right angles to the first layer in a grid pattern ②. Check that the second layer is totally level. You are now ready to begin laying out ③.

Laying out

The framing bed now acts as a map for the caravan frames. Mark a centre line using a chalk line. Then mark the positions of the corner posts of the frame 3ft 3in (99cm) each side of the centre line. Lay out the posts on the framing bed and secure in place with ratchet straps. Attach a dummy ridge pole to the framing bed. This is the same diameter as the ridge pole that will be used in the caravan. Lay the cruck poles out so that their butt ends are inside the corner posts and the tops pass each side of the dummy cruck ④.

The frame laid out on the framing bed. Notice the dummy ridge pole in place.

Marking an orientation line on the end of a cruck pole.

Beginning to saw down to the level line.

Sawing down to the level line on one of the cruck poles. Note the saw cut is inside the scribe line. It is easier to take more out later than to create a baggy joint!

The half-lap joint

The first joint is a basic half-lap joint where the cruck poles cross. Lay one cruck pole over the other where they meet the dummy ridge pole and then chock the top cruck pole at the base end, so that the pole sits level over the opposing cruck pole. It will be chocked up by the same amount as the diameter of the lower cruck pole it is resting on. Draw orientation marks on the end of each pole with a small spirit level and pencil (5). These marks are essential to ensure that the pole is in the correct orientation when the joint is cut.

Mark lines with a pencil where one pole crosses the other from on top and underneath. Lift off the top pole and secure it to the framing bed, ensuring the orientation mark is level. Measure down half the amount of the height you chocked up the cruck by (half the diameter of the lower cruck pole) and mark a level line on both sides of the cruck pole, do the same on the other cruck.

Saw down to the level lines on each of the cruck poles using a panel saw, following the lines you drew where one pole overlaps the other (6). Add an extra saw cut in the middle to make chiselling out the joint easier. Chisel out to the level lines on each pole and offer the poles together. Small adjustments are usually necessary to get them to sit down snugly and get contact between the two level surfaces at the base of the joint (7), (8).

Offering the two halves of the half-lap joint to each other.

Setting up the scriber, using the level board.

Drawing the level line to cut through the scribe.

Scribing the profile of one log onto another.

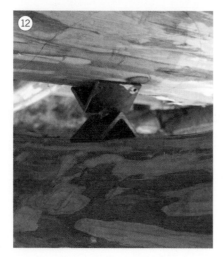

The finished scribe.

The butterpat joint

Lay the lower and upper tie beams across the cruck and corner poles to begin scribing the butterpat joint (see measurements in the diagram on page 111). Once in place, lift the beams and place on scribing pods. Draw orientation marks on each end. Measure the radius of the smallest pole laid out on the framing bed and add on the height of the scribing pod. This measurement will be the distance between the points on the scribing tool. Open up the scribing tool and set the points to this distance, then take the scribing tool to the level board and, with both points on the level line on the level board, adjust both bubbles on the scribing tool so that they are level ⑨. You are now ready to begin scribing. The level board must be level in all directions. At any point during scribing the scribing points can be readjusted to a different position, provided the gap between them is the same as the original distance between the points on the scribing tool and you return to the level board and reset the bubbles on the scribing tool.

Scribing itself takes a little practice. The process involves transferring the profiled curve of one log onto the other. If scribing the tie-beam where it meets the corner post, the spike of the scribing tool will be placed touching the corner post while the pencil will touch the tie-beam. At the same time, both bubbles on the scribing tool must be reading level. Begin to move the tool across the poles, keeping the bubbles level at all times and a curved profile will appear on the tie beam. Continue all the way around the log. Once the scribe is complete, draw a level line on each side of the tie-beam, which cuts through the scribe line about a third of the way up the scribe measuring from the bottom of the log. This marks the top of the cog.

A line at the same height needs to be drawn on the opposite side of the tie-beam, this can be done by measuring up off the framing bed or by using the scribing tool as a level. To do this, put the point of the scribing tool on the position where the level line meets the curve of the scribe. With both bubbles reading level, mark the corner post below. Using a boat level, draw a level line from that point to reach the opposite side of the tie-beam. Put the scribe point on the line you have drawn and with both bubbles level, mark where the pencil meets the scribe line. Draw a level line that cuts through both sides of the scribe line ⑩. You will have successfully transferred a level line from one side of the log to another ⑪. Using the boat level, make orientation marks from the tie-beam down to the corner posts, so that after chiselling the joint you can return it to the exact position where you scribed the joint ⑫.

With all the joints scribed along the tie beam, lift it off the scribing pods and secure it to the frame with ratchet straps or timber dogs, making sure that the orientation line on the end of the tie-beam is plumb, although it will be upside down. Join the points where the level lines meet the scribe lines and then saw down to the level lines. Using a chisel and slick create a flat face between the level lines. Draw two parallel lines, which will form the cog in the joint. Make the cog as large as possible but ensure you have heartwood for the cog, not sapwood. Using a curved gouge, score out the scribe line and remove the excess wood working back towards the mark of the cog. Using a straight chisel, create a right angle from the top of the cog to meet the curved profile you are chiselling with the gouge (13), (14).

Fitting the joints

With the joints completed in the tie-beam, place it back in its original position on top of the crucks and corner posts. Make sure all the orientation marks are correct, then mark where the edges of the cog meet the crucks and corner posts and measure the distance from the highest point of the now chiselled-out scribe line to the bottom of the cog. This is the depth to saw down into the corner posts and crucks. Measure each one individually as they will vary. Saw where you have marked the edges of the cogs to the measured depth and chisel out to a flat surface and then lower the cog into the corner posts and crucks until there is a snug fit and the cog has disappeared and the scribe line has come smoothly onto the pole it was transferred from (15), (16).

The butter-pat joint chiselled out. The right-angled cog (the butter) sits in the curved 'butter dish'.

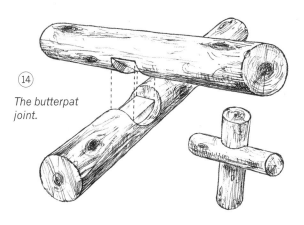

The butterpat joint.

Lowering the tie-beam with butterpat cog on a corner post.

The completed butterpat joint.

Tips
for joint making

For joints where you can't see how well the internal parts fit together, leaves can be used to help identify any parts that don't sit together well. Lay a few leaves in the bottom part of the joint and lower the cog onto them. Any high patches that need more chiselling will be clearly marked with green chlorophyll. Chisel them off and you should get a snug fit.

Using leaves to highlight any tight areas within the joint.

The green areas on the butter-pat cog are highlighted by the chlorophyll in the leaves.

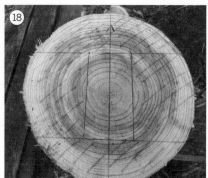

A chalk line gives a level line in a round pole from which to measure from and is used to centralize the position of the tenon.

Transfering the tenon markings to the top of the post. The chalk line is marked with an arrow and runs through the centre of the tenon, the shaded areas are to be removed and the lines which reach the edge of the post are to be transferred down to the shoulder line.

A completed tenon.

Cutting the tenons

While the frame is still on the framing bed, this is the time to cut the tenons on the corner posts. Following the layout plan, measure up to find the correct location for the shoulder of the tenon. The shoulders on each side should be at the same level. This can be checked by measuring from your marks on the framing bed. A laser level can be a useful addition at this point as the laser will position a line onto the curve of the roundwood, which can then be drawn over with a pencil. This helps assist in cutting a level shoulder on the post. A chalk line should be pinged along the length of the post and this can be used to help centralize the position of the tenon (17).

I cut the tenons on roundwood frames to a standard 4 x 2 x 4in (10 x 5 x 10cm). With the shoulder marked, measure 4in (10cm) up from the shoulder and cut off the end of the post. Using the chalk line as the centre of the tenon, and by using a small carpenter's square, it is possible to mark out the profile of the tenon on the end grain of the post. Transfer these lines back down the round post to where the shoulder is marked (18). The shoulder can now be cut and, if the grain is straight, the waste wood can be chiselled from the marks on the top of the post to remove it. If the grain is not straight or there are knots, it is better to rip saw the waste wood down to the shoulder so as to ensure a square tenon (19).

Next, the frame must be drilled and pegged and each peg individually wedged at both ends to ensure there is no movement in the joints. See pages 122–123 for details of making pegs.

Attaching the frames to the chassis

The next step is to transfer the frames and attach them to the chassis. I used 6 x 6in (150 x 150mm) sawn Douglas fir beams and bolted this to the chassis as shown in the measurement diagram on page 111. Place a central string line down the chassis and measure out from this in the same way the framing bed was measured at the beginning . I then marked the position of where the corner posts will meet the Douglas fir beams. Lift the frames into position (mechanical assistance is recommended for this, or a lot of friends) so that the corner posts line up with the marks on the Douglas fir beams. Having checked the tie-beams are level, draw lines where the corner posts and cruck posts meet the Douglas fir beams. Saw into the corner posts and crucks to a depth of 1½in (38mm) and chisel out a flat surface then offer them up to Douglas fir beams so that the frame slides over the beams . Fix with stainless-steel timber locks or coach screws. Fix temporary bracing to support frames in an upright position until the wall plates and ridge pole are connected.

Cut tenons on the intermediate posts and fix them to the Douglas fir beams in the same way as the corner and cruck posts, using the layout in the measurement diagram on page 111. The ridge pole can now be offered into position between the horns of the crucks and once in position, drill and peg it into both cruck poles (using 1in /25mm pegs). The lower tie-beam can now have the central section cut out to become an interrupted tie-beam to allow access to the doorway (see pictures 25 and 34).

The wall plates can now be worked while positioned on two level carpenter's trestles. Draw a level line across one end using a boat level and stretch the chalk line from one end of the log to the other, lift the chalk line in the middle, let go and it will ping a chalk line down the log to the other end. Another level line is drawn across and another chalk line pinged up the opposing side of the log so that the level lines meet 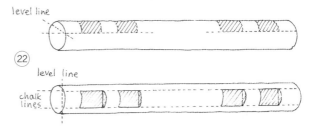. Measure and mark the positions of where the tenons on top of the posts will meet the wall plate and chisel out flats in these positions by removing wood between the two chalk lines on the wall plate . Offer up the wall plates and lay them on top of the posts so that the flats are on top of the tenons. The exact position of the tenons can now be marked, the wall plate placed back on the carpenter's trestles and the mortises cut. Drill the mortises to remove some of the wood and then chisel them out 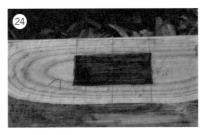. A corner chisel can be a useful addition to ensure the right angles run true to the bottom of the mortise. Lift the wall plates into position and lower them onto the tenons. These are then drilled and pegged using ⅝in (16mm) pegs .

The chassis with centre string line and Douglas fir beams attached.

Detail of a corner-post joint with Douglas fir beam.

Marking out a wall plate for cutting the mortises.

Level chalk lines between which the flats are cut for the mortises.

A mortise cut into the wall plate.

The frames attached to the chassis with ridge pole and wall plates in place; note diagonal bracing still in position.

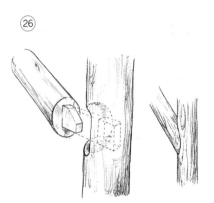

(26)

Knee brace with mortise-and-tenon joint.

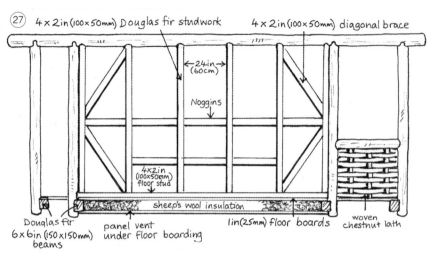

(27) 4 x 2in (100 x 50mm) Douglas fir studwork

4 x 2in (100 x 50mm) diagonal brace

←24in→ (60cm)

Noggins

4 x 2in (100 x 50mm) floor stud

sheep's wool insulation

Douglas fir 6 x 6in (150 x 150mm) beams

panel vent under floor boarding

1in (25mm) floor boards

woven chestnut lath

A cross-section of the caravan showing diagonal bracing in the studwork.

Finishing the construction

At this stage there are a number of options on how you complete the project, many of which are more conventional construction techniques. The first is to ensure there is some diagonal bracing in the frame to reduce racking. This can be done by fitting knee braces between the corner posts and wall plates as I would on a larger roundwood frame (26). (If you are choosing this option, be sure to cut the mortise for the brace in the wall plate at the same time as cutting the mortises for the posts.) I chose to fit the bracing into the studwork between the intermediate posts. Place the opposing diagonal braces at each end of the row of wall studwork (27).

First the subfloor needs to be screwed to the Douglas fir beams. Cut out the panelvent (or your chosen subfloor) to fill in all the space between the two internal Douglas fir beams. Fit the floor joists at 16in (400mm) centres and either fit with joist hangers or notch into the Douglas fir beams. Fill the gaps between the joists with sheep's-wool insulation (28) and then nail the 6 x 1in (150 x 25mm) western red cedar floorboards to the floor joists using stainless steel or silicon bronze 2½in (65mm) ring shanks. Attach a floor stud on top of the floorboards between the intermediate posts (make sure you allow for thickness of baton and cladding to the outside of the stud and internal wall boarding on the inside when positioning this stud). The 4 x 2in (100 x 50mm) studs are then nailed to the floor stud and notched in and nailed to the wall plate above. Space the studs at 24in (60cm) centres and fix diagonal bracing in end bays to reduce racking. Noggins can be fitted to stabilize studs. Try to position noggins so that they are in the right place to fix your chosen internal boarding onto.

Any window frames should be positioned in the studwork at this point. The position of these will depend on your chosen internal layout. I like to consider where I will be sleeping and sitting and position windows accordingly. I used some conventional windows salvaged from a local building project but time taken to make more attractive windows would improve the overall aesthetic of the caravan.

Attach a breathable waterproof membrane onto the outside of the studwork and on the outside of this fix vertical 2 x 1in (50 x 25mm) batons to the studwork, sandwiching the membrane. Fix the cladding to the batons, ensuring angled cuts on the end grain to get a tight fit where the cladding meets the roundwood corner posts. I have used waney-edge cladding. Ensure there is an overlap of the boards of around 2in (50mm) to allow for shrinkage. On the inside of the caravan the walls are insulated with sheep's wool between the studwork and then the finished walling material, which could be tongue-and-groove timber or, as in this project, I have used panelvent and a breathable clay paint (29).

(28)

Sheep's wool breathable insulation between floor joists.

(29)

Internal walls with a clay-paint finish showing the exposed ridge pole and wall plate.

Looking up to the sawn rafter ends with fascia board attached.

Roundwood rafters over the porch and wood store at each end of the caravan add to the rustic appeal.

The wood store ensures a good supply of dry fuel to keep the caravan warm on the coldest of winter nights.

Finishing touches

Space the 4 x 2in (100 x 50mm) roof rafters at 2ft (60cm) centres. These can be let into the ridge pole and wall plate by differing amounts depending on the taper of the poles. Offer up the rafter and draw a pencil line each side of it, sawing down the pencil lines to the required depth and chiselling out the waste wood, making sure to keep the angle the same as the roof pitch. A sliding bevel can be useful for this. I like to run a string line across the length of the roof and work my rafters to this to keep a level line along the roof. Fix the rafters with timber locks (impact driver hexagonal-headed screws) to ensure a strong fit ③⓪.

Over the porch and wood store I used roundwood rafters to keep the round aesthetic of the frames on show ③①, ③②. On top of the sawn rafters, I attached a breathable waterproof membrane and on top of that cross batons on which I fitted the onduline sheeting. A fascia board closes off the rafter feet and a roof light window adds a lot of extra light to the caravan and a good view of the stars from the bed.

The door is made from the western red cedar floorboards and has cover strips vertically over the joints in the boards ③③. The deck is edged with sweet chestnut lath (see page 98) and woven in the same technique as the woven panel in chapter three (see page 50) ③④.

The finished caravan with ladder steps access as it is parked on a slope. The scissor jacks for adjusting the height are welded to the chassis.

The door and chestnut handrail with split chestnut lath infill.

A roundwood caravan blending into the surroundings that it was built from.

PEG MAKING

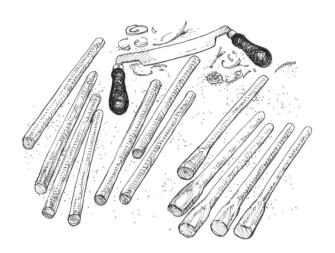

Pegs are a very important fixing in timber-framed buildings as they help keep the joints together. The predominant species used to make them is oak, as it is structurally strong and metal fixings corrode if used with oak or sweet chestnut frames because the tannic acid in the wood reacts with the metal. The type of peg varies depending on the timber frame being constructed. The majority of green oak timber framing uses a tapered peg whereas roundwood timber framing uses a wedged cylindrical peg.

To make
TAPERED PEGS

Materials you will need
A log of green oak: the same length that you need the pegs to be

Recommended tools
Froe, maul, draw knife, shaving horse.

A tapered peg is made from green oak by first splitting the round oak into smaller segments using a froe and maul (1). Once a segment is split down to a small piece, transfer it to the shaving horse (see page 202) and work with a draw knife (2) to create a tapered peg of about 1in (25mm) at the thicker end (3).

Splitting the oak down into smaller sections with the froe.

Shaping the peg on the shaving horse with a draw knife.

The completed peg, ready to be hammered into a timber-frame joint.

DRAW PEGGING

One technique often used in green oak frames in England, but less in the US, is draw pegging or draw boring, where the holes drilled through the tenon are offset by about 1/8in (3mm) from those drilled through the mortise. This process allows the joint to be pulled tightly together as the tapered peg works its way through the offset holes.

To make
CYLINDRICAL PEGS

Materials you will need
Straight grained, sawn air-dried oak blank:
1¹/₄in (32mm) x 1¹/₄in (32mm) by the length of peg you need

Recommended tools
Draw knife, shaving horse, rounding (rotary) plane, vice, Japanese saw.

A cylindrical peg is made from shaving the edges of the air-dried square section of oak on a shaving horse (see page 202) with a draw knife, so that it fits into the wider end of the rounding plane. The rounding planes are fixed sizes and I use 1in (25mm) and ⁵/₈in (16mm) rounding planes. The 1in (25mm) pegs are used for making butterpat joints and the ⁵/₈in (16mm) for pegging tenons on knee braces. Shaving an air-dried section of oak is a very different experience to shaving greenwood, so ensure your draw knife is very sharp and take small sections off the oak at a time. Work until the peg blank is even all the way down and will fit into the rounding plane. Fit the blank into a vice and rotate the rounding plane like a giant pencil sharpener to produce an even, cylindrical peg (1). Leave the end of the peg fatter to assist with knocking it into the hole. Insert an oak wedge into the opposite end by rip sawing through the centre of the end grain of the peg with a Japanese saw (2), (3).

The rounding plane converting the shaved-oak blank into a 1in (25mm) cylindrical peg.

The wedged end of the peg.

A selection of finished pegs.

CORDWOOD
WALLING

Cordwood walling is a simple but attractive style of construction that I have used on a few buildings. It is best to use durable softwoods as they have better insulation value than hardwoods. This technique is a great use for poor-quality thinnings or wind-thrown trees.

Materials you will need
Seasoned softwood logs
Clay, straw, sand or lime: for the pug mixture

Recommended tools
Chainsaw, pointing trowel, spirit level, shovel, axe, plastic tarpaulin, string line, long spirit level.

Preparing the foundation and the logs

Some form of base or foundation at the bottom of the wall is recommended. I use brick rubble or scalpings and, depending on the soil type, scrape away the topsoil and compact the rubble to form a solid base.

The length of the cordwood will determine the thickness of your wall. I have often used 18in (46cm) lengths, which work well. Cross cut the cordwood to the same length. If the logs are of a large diameter then splitting them down with an axe will help.

Making the pug mixture

The next stage is to make up a suitable pug mixture for infilling the wall (I do not believe in using cement). It is important to allow for the fact that the wood is likely to shrink as it dries out so a clay-based mixture is most suitable. The actual formula for this pug mixture will depend on the soil type you have available. If you are fortunate enough to have a clay-based subsoil with a reasonable sand content then adding some chopped straw as a fibrous binding material may be all you need to do. If your soil is heavy clay then adding some sand as well as the chopped straw will help reduce cracking during the drying process.

The best method for mixing the pug is to lay down a plastic tarpaulin and shovel your clay and sand onto it. Add water and work the pug to a thick, but pliable, consistency – something akin to porridge. Add handfuls of chopped straw and work these into the mixture. An effective way to mix the pug is to take off your shoes and socks and work the pug with your feet. After a while, use the tarpaulin to help mix the pug by lifting one end and rolling the mixture back onto itself, then get back in and work with your feet (1).

Constructing the wall

Once the pug is ready for use, shovel a layer on top of the rubble foundation and begin to lay out your first logs. A string line can be useful to keep the wall straight (if that is your intention) and, as you start to build up, a long spirit level is useful to ensure the wall is not leaning and stays vertical. Add more pug on top of and between each layer and keep adding the logs (2). Try to choose logs that are a good fit to ensure that there are not any large areas of pug in the wall. If you are building a wall with a good roof overhang (recommended with this style of walling) then the clay pug will be all you need. Once the wall is completed, a pointing trowel can be used to neatly finish the pug around the end grain of the walls. Expect some cracking and that you may need to repoint a second time after a couple of months. If your wall is to be very exposed it is worth pointing the wall with a mixture of sand and lime putty at a ratio of 3½:1. When adding the pug be sure to leave a gap at the end of each log on the exposed end to allow room to point in the lime at a later date once the wall has settled (3).

Mixing the pug on a tarpaulin with the cordwood wall construction under way.

Cordwood wall nearing completion.

LEFT: Completed cordwood wall.
BELOW: A cordwood bothy.

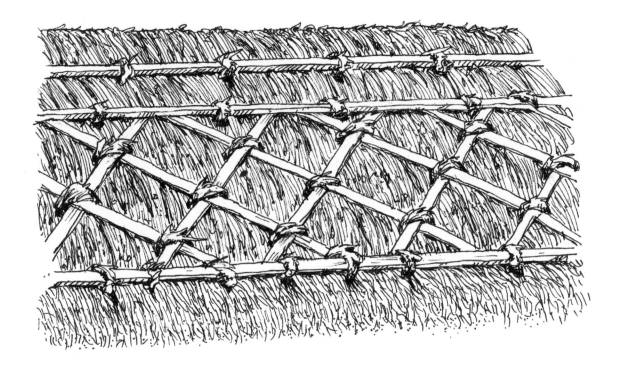

THATCHING SPARS

Thatching is the traditional roofing of buildings with straw and vegetative material, which goes back to the Bronze Age in Britain. This traditional roofing method continues to the current day and needs coppiced materials to hold it in place. The thatch is secured in place by a long horizontal stick of hazel, in the round or cleft, known as a sway, which is then secured in place by the twisted spars. This holds the underthatch in place. Another layer is then placed on top and held in place in the same way.

More layers are placed, working steadily up the roof to the desired thickness of thatch. The exterior of the thatch is finished with liggers and again stapled in place with the spars.

Materials you will need

Rods of hazel: approximately $1^1/_4$–$2^1/_2$in (32–63mm) in diameter

Recommended tools

Spar hook (small billhook), riving knife.

Splitting the hazel into two with a spar hook.

Splitting the halves into thinner spars.

Split spars ready for pointing.

Using a bench and riving knife to split spars.

Cut the hazel to the length that the thatcher wants the spars – this is usually 2–2ft 6in (60–76cm). The rods need to be straight and free of knots. Start with the thin end and tap the spar hook into the end of the hazel and work it down the rod (1). The rods are short so run-out is unlikely on the first cleave. Next, take one of the cleft rods and repeat the process using the spar hook to open the split (2). Twist the hook to and fro and use your thumb as a guide behind the hook to control the split (3). The standard cleaving rule applies: if the cleave starts going off to one side, applying pressure to the thicker part will cause the split to return to the centre. Some spar makers find it easier to use a bench and riving knife and work the hazel through the blade (4).

You should get between 6 to 16 spars from each cut section of the rod, depending on the thickness. The spars are then pointed at each end and bundled tight. The thatcher will twist each spar to turn it into a staple as he works along the roof (5).

A twisted spar.

GIANT STAPLES

Spars, gads, broaches, spics, splints, speekes, spikes, spits, speaks, sparrows, sparrods, sprees, tangs, spelks, brotches, privets, pricks, withy-necks, ledgers, roovers, scolp, scollop, sgilb, scob, scope, scoup and scrobe. These are some of the many names these curious but simple 'giant staples' of the thatcher's world have been known by, according to Edlin's *Woodland Crafts in Britain*. I have always known them as spars or gads but regional variations are common in craft produce.

Spars and liggers holding down the top layer of thatch.

Spars visible on the finished edge of the roof.

YURT

For centuries, the yurt has been the portable home of choice throughout central Asia. The circular design and lightweight poles make it strong enough to be able to withstand strong winds and yet be light enough for ease of transportation. The rise in popularity of the yurt in Europe has been a growing trend over the past 15 years and there are many established yurt makers plying their trade across the continent. I have made a number of yurts over the years and lived in one at Prickly Nut Wood nearly 20 years ago. The yurt can be insulated and fitted with a stove and is therefore suitable for most climates.

Recommended tools

Draw knife, spokeshave, bow saw, cordless drill, 3/16in (4.5mm) drill bit, 1in (25mm) auger bit, sand paper, calipers, steam-bending equipment, gauntlets, clamps (lots), copper soldering iron, froe, shaving horse, cleaving brake, sewing machine (domestic or industrial).

OPPOSITE: Peeling sweet chestnut with a draw knife.

Materials you will need

To make a 16ft (4.9m)-diameter bentwood yurt. Best materials are coppiced ash or sweet chestnut.
78 (allow 80) rods for the trellis or wall poles: 6ft 6in (1.98m) long x 1¼in (32mm) diameter
38 (allow 40) rods for the roof ribs: 8ft 6in (2.6m) long x 1½in (38mm) diameter
1 rod for the door lintel: 3ft (90cm) long x 3in (75mm) diameter
1 rod for the threshold: 3ft (90cm) long x 5in (125mm) diameter
2 rods for the door uprights: 6ft 6in (1.98m) long x 2in (50mm)
1 rod for the crown: 15ft (4.5m) long x 5in (125mm)
10 rods for the crown bracing: 5ft (1.5m) lengths x 1in (25mm) diameter
Nylon cord: 80yds (73m) of ⅛in (3mm) diameter
Rope: 27yd (25m) of ⅝in (16mm) diameter
Boiled linseed oil/thinners

For the cover
Fireproof and waterproof canvas: 82sq yds (75sq m) of 12 or 14oz (340 or 396g)
Eyelets: approximately 50 at ⅝in (16mm) diameter
Paper: for templates of the roof
Ties or hook-and-loop tape straps: for securing the roll-up door
PVC: for a skirt around the base (optional)

Barney Farrell and Tom Baker with bundles of coppiced sweet chestnut yurt poles at Prickly Nut Wood.

Making the wall trellis

Select poles that are straight and have minimal knots ①. The poles all need to be peeled with a draw knife and then further finished with a spokeshave (a concave spokeshave can be useful). The poles can be used without steaming but if you are looking for the traditional bowed curve of a Mongolian 'ger' (yurt) then steaming the poles for half an hour and placing them in a bending jig will create the shape ②, ③. See page 182 for steam-bending instructions. The next stage is to drill out the poles. For this you need to set out a marking jig. A length of baton with the hole positions marked on it works well ④. Drill the first hole 3in (75mm) from the bottom of the pole and then six further holes at 1ft (30cm) intervals leaving

3in (75mm) at the top to form the horns ⑤. Sand the trellis poles and then oil them with a thinned-down boiled linseed oil ⑥. The trellis can now be tied together with the nylon cord to form the pattern ⑦. Where the poles cross over, the holes should approximately line up. Tie a knot in one end of a short length of cord and thread through a hole. The knot will stop it pulling through completely. Pass the cord through the other hole and tie it off with a half-hitch knot. The trellis will need to be in three or four sections so it can be rolled up into a bundle and then unrolled and unfolded out into a trellis panel. Where the trellis sections join one another, the end poles will need to overlap with the next section and be tied together with cord.

(2) *The trellis-bending jig.*

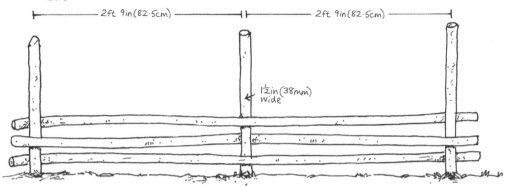

|← 2ft 9in(82·5cm) →|← 2ft 9in(82·5cm) →|

1½in(38mm) wide

(3) *The trellis-bending jig from above.*

(4)

Drilling out the trellis poles using a piece of baton as a marking gauge.

(5) *Distances for drilling the trellis.*

3in (75mm) 1ft 3in (37·5cm) 2ft 3in (67·5cm) 3ft 3in (97·5cm) 4ft 3in (127·5cm) 5ft 3in (157·5cm) 6ft 3in (187·5cm) 6ft 6in (198cm)

(6)

A thorough sanding of the poles produces a fine finish prior to oiling with thinned boiled linseed oil.

(7) *The trellis pattern.*

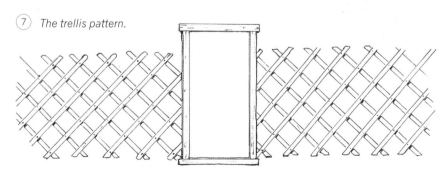

Boil bending the roof ribs in an oil drum.

The roof ribs

I boil bend rather than steam bend my roof ribs as I have a large enough bending jig for them all to fit in one batch. I have a 45-gallon (205 litre) steel drum from which I have ground out the top. This is raised up with a couple of rows of loose bricks that form a firebox. The bricks have air gaps and an open front in which to insert wood. A piece of plywood can be rested over the top to form a lid and speed up the boiling. Once the water is boiled, remove the plywood lid and insert the poles with the butt ends into the water. Most of the pole is not in the boiling water but the section that is immersed is the part that will be bent around the log in the jig. Boil the poles for about one hour ⑧.

The jig I use is made up of a chestnut log that blew over in the hurricane of 1987. The log is about 20in (51cm) in diameter with a plank fixed behind it, secured using long pegs hammered into the ground. This plank takes a lot of pressure and needs to be very well secured. An 8 x 3in (200 x 75mm) plank would be ideal ⑨. Tie the top end of the roof rib to a horizontal pole, which is again secured firmly into the ground. Wearing gauntlets, as the pole will be hot, push the butt end over the log and tuck it behind the plank. Bend the poles over the log and tie them onto the horizontal pole with bailer twine. Once they are all in the jig, leave them for about a week before releasing ⑩. It is good to slightly 'overbend' them as they will move slightly out of their bent position once released.

Peel the poles and then sand them down. Each pole then needs a tenon made on the top end. Create a ¾ x ¾in (19 x 19mm) tenon about 4in (100mm) in length. Check the square section with calipers and then take off a spokeshave's worth all the way round ⑪. The roof ribs can now be oiled with thinned boiled linseed oil.

⑨ *The bending jig for the roof ribs.*

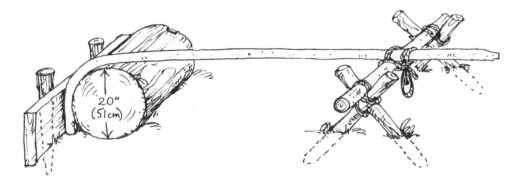

Bending the roof ribs over a jig made from a large tree trunk.

Squaring off the ends of the roof rib to form a tenon, which will fit through the square mortise holes in the yurt crown.

The crown

Look for a very straight pole 15ft (4.5m) long and about 5in (125mm) in diameter. I like to choose a pole with no major knots and that has been cut fresh on the morning I am making the hoop. Steam bending is the ultimate manipulation of wood – a strong straight pole growing in the wood in the morning can become a rigid circular hoop by the evening. Peel the pole and cleave it with a froe and a cleaving brake (see page 202). Cleaving a 15ft (4.5m) pole should be done with care. It is a long length to keep the cleave straight and avoid it running out, hence the importance of selecting a knot-free straight pole to begin with. Most yurt makers use two pieces of timber to make the crown and scarf them together. This is a successful method and means that you only need to cleave an 8ft (2.4m) length into two and will need a smaller steam box. However, for me, part of the appeal is creating a 360-degree hoop from one piece of wood. Take one of the lengths and work the cleft face smooth with a draw knife and shaving horse (see page 202) ⑫. Turn the wood over and work the curved face down, using calipers to check it becomes an even 1in (25mm) thick all the way along its length ⑬.

Using a draw knife and a shaving horse to shape the cleft chestnut pole into a 1 x 4in (25 x 100mm) shaven plank for the steamer.

Using calipers to check the thickness.

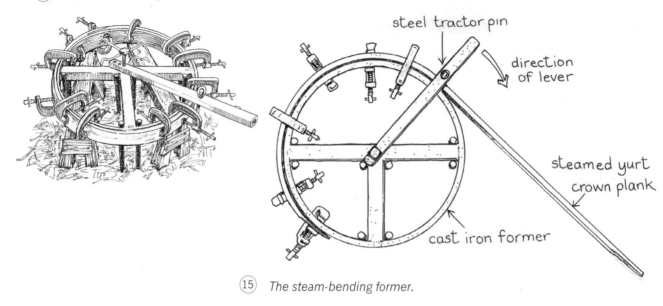

(14) *The steam-bending former.*

steel tractor pin

direction of lever

steamed yurt crown plank

cast iron former

(15) *The steam-bending former.*

Next, taper the ends for the scarf joint. Taper the last 18in (450mm) of each end of the plank from 1in (25mm) down to ¼in (6mm). Make sure you taper the opposing sides of each end of the shaven plank so that they meet as they curve around the former (see picture 17). Once the steamer is steaming well, place the shaven plank in the steam box and keep a constant flow of steam for three hours (see also page 182).

Set up and prepare for the bending process. You will need to find at least one other person, lots of clamps and some good gauntlets as the wood will be very hot when it comes out of the steamer. Carry the steaming wood as quickly as possible to the former and clamp one end to it. I use an old iron cartwheel mould with welded bracing across the centre. I also drill two 1in (25mm) holes through the former so I can get a fixing through the scarf joint before releasing it from the former. Make sure the first clamp fixes one tapered end of the wood over the hole and then begin bending and clamping. The bending should be slow but constant, with your assistant

clamping at regular intervals. Due to the length of the wood and the forces involved, I use a long lever, which is fitted into the centre of the former with a steel tractor pin. There is a second steel tractor pin that guides the wood to the former as I walk around it with the lever (14), (15). This gives extra assistance and ensures the wood is pressed tight against the former. This whole process from taking the wood out of the steamer to reaching the clamped crown (16) should take about three minutes. Now you can relax and allow the crown to cool and the fibres to reset in their new position.

The following day fix the scarf joint together (17). I use a couple of small bolts that can be fitted while the crown is still on the former through the 1in (25mm) hole. Release the clamps and slowly ease the crown off the former. If you don't want to use steel bolts to hold the clamp together it can be done with small pegs. You will need to angle the pegs through the scarf joint in opposing directions. I would recommend two pegs in each direction.

(16)

The yurt crown, steam bent in one piece and clamped around the 4ft (1.2m)-diameter iron former.

(17)

The scarf joint for the crown.

Fitting the bracing in the crown.

The copper soldering iron.

Measure the circumference of the crown and then work out the spacing distances of the 38 roof ribs. Mark their positions on the crown. Then mark out the positions for the bracing. The bracing should be positioned so that the holes are midway between the roof pole mortises. The bracing pole holes should be angled down slightly whereas the roof mortises need an upward angle of about 28 degrees to allow for the angle that the roof ribs will enter the crown. Bend the bracing poles into their holes and allow them to create a raised dome. This will be the highest point of the yurt and the cover will be angled downwards from this point. The bracing strengthens the crown (18). You can now drill the roof mortises at the 28-degree angle (each yurt will have minor differences). I use a ³/₄in (19mm) auger bit and then heat up a ³/₄in (19mm) square copper soldering iron (19) and push this through the round hole. The soldering iron burns out the corners and leaves a square mortise (20). This process is much faster than chiselling and takes away the stresses on the bent wood that chiselling can cause. It also nicely seals the cut wood inside the mortise (21), (22).

The door frame

Door frames can be as simple or elaborate as you wish. I lived in a yurt with oak double doors and therefore it needed a substantial frame. A strong frame can also help when tensioning the wall band. A lightweight door frame allows for ease of transportation and the door is often canvas, attached to the cover and can be rolled up and secured at the lintel of the frame. This is the type of door frame described here.

First cleave the threshold and work it with a draw knife to create a rustic plank. Then peel and draw knife the upright poles and taper the ends. Using a rounding plane, create a 1in (25mm) circular tenon at each end. Peel and draw knife the lintel and then drill 1in (25mm) holes into the threshold and lintel 2in (50mm) in from the ends.

The heated soldering iron burning the round hole into a square mortise.

The ³/₄in (19mm) mortises burnt through the crown with the copper soldering iron.

Looking up through a completed crown.

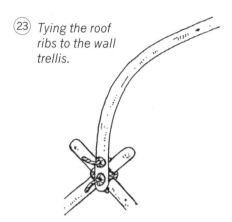

(23) *Tying the roof ribs to the wall trellis.*

The butt ends of the roof ribs are tied between the trellis horns.

The yurt frame raised.

Erecting the yurt

If the yurt is intended for long-term use, a raised timber platform is recommended. Otherwise choose a level piece of ground and knock a peg with a nail half hammered into the top in the centre. Attach a piece of string to the nail and measure 8ft (2.4m). You can now walk around in a circle and see exactly where the yurt trellis will sit.

Open up the trellis and allow it to stand in its approximate position. Stand up the door frame and tie the trellis to the door frame pole using a clove hitch knot and nylon cord. Join the sections of trellis together using the nylon cord and then attach the last section to the opposing door frame. Push out the trellis to make sure the diamonds in the pattern are square and then check for a true circle using the string in the central peg.

Next, fit the wall tension band. This is a structural part of the yurt and ensures that the junction between the roof rafters and the top of the trellis is kept in place and the rafters cannot push the trellis out. The band is usually about 12in (30cm) wide and is secured by attaching it to holes drilled through the door frame. (For temporarily checking how a yurt frame fits together, a rope will suffice and the optional use of webbing and a ratchet strap ensures greater control over the tension.)

With the help of an assistant, take the crown and three roof ribs into the centre of the yurt. Tie the first roof rib to the first pair of trellis 'horns' next to the door (23), (24). Count one third of the way around the trellis horns and attach the second roof rib. Slot these two roof ribs into their corresponding mortises on the crown. Count around another third on the crown and insert the third roof rib into the mortise. Carefully lift the crown into the air. I find a second person pushing the crown steadily upwards using a rake helps! Tie the third roof rib to the trellis horns in its corresponding position. Now attach the rest of the ribs, working evenly around the yurt. The shorter ribs fit into the top of the door frame (25).

An example of a canvas cover.

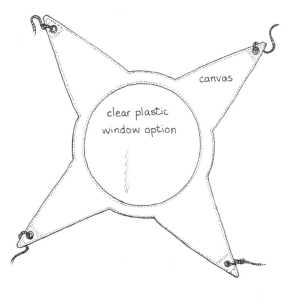

(27) *Canvas crown cover.*

canvas

clear plastic
window option

The cover

For the cover (26), use a fireproof and waterproof 12 or 14oz (340 or 396g) canvas. The sewing can be done on a domestic sewing machine but an industrial machine makes the job easier. Firstly, make the tension band that runs from door frame to door frame, about 12in (300mm) wide and with eyelets at each end.

The wall section is made by measuring the circumference of the yurt, door frame to door frame, and making a piece that runs from the trellis horns to the ground. Attaching a PVC skirt along the bottom will help with longevity. Attach eyelets along the top for attaching to the trellis horns and down the sides to attach to the door frames. Consider any plastic windows you may choose to add.

The roof cover is best made from interlocking triangles of canvas. Make up paper templates and lay them over the roof. Follow the profile so that the template covers three roof poles at a time. Allow a bit extra to overlap the trellis horns and make sure the tops fit tightly over the crown, leaving the inner circle

open. Eyelets will be needed all around the wider bottom edge to pull the canvas down tight. These can be roped down to pegs on the ground. The top should stay tensioned against the rim of the crown.

Make the crown cover by creating a four-pointed canvas star (27). The centre must overlap the crown and the top of the roof cover by about 6in (150mm). The centre can be plastic, which gives good light to the yurt and allows star gazing at night in winter. However, you may prefer to make it out of pure canvas and remove the crown cover totally on dry days. Eyelets are attached in the point of each star for roping down securely.

A canvas door that rolls up can be made by sewing a round of wood into the bottom of the door as a weight. Ties or hook-and-loop tape straps will secure it when rolled up. If you are using the yurt for long-term use in one place, a solid wood door is recommended.

DOMESTIC CRAFTS

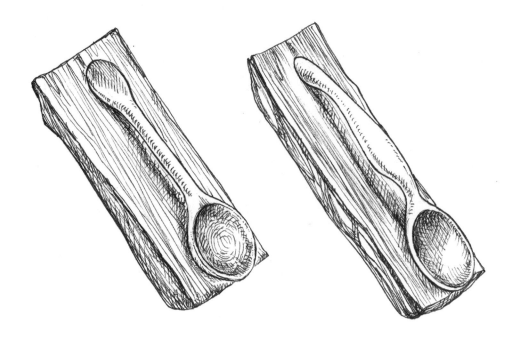

SPOON CARVING

At a basic level, all you need is a small pocket knife, an offcut from a branch in the garden and a bit of imagination and you can whittle away until you have a spoon. There are a wide range of spoon-carving styles with specialist designs, shapes and patterns. Here I will look at a couple of techniques. One involves using a pole lathe to turn a spoon blank and the other looks at the more free-form technique of working from a small log or from a curved branch, often referred to as the Swedish style.

Materials you will need

A length of roundwood long enough for your desired spoon: Suitable species are sycamore, birch, maple, cherry, lime, rowan and alder. Many species can be used for spoon carving but it is best to avoid woods with a high tannin content if they are to be used for culinary purposes.
Olive or walnut oil

Recommended tools

Pocket carving knife, bent carving knife (hooked knife), curved gouge, minijarn gouge, froe, side axe, pole lathe, clamps, sandpaper.

To make a spoon
USING A POLE LATHE

Turning the blank on a pole lathe.

First, choose the length of wood for the spoon, split the log in two and rough it out using a small side axe. Once the blank is shaped enough to work on the pole lathe (see page 202), turn the wood until it resembles ①. Use a small froe to split the blank in half ②. You will now have two spoon blanks ready to work using hand tools ③. Use a carving knife and a bent carving knife for the bowl. As the shape is already defined by the work of the pole lathe, it is possible to make a regular set of spoons this way if desired. To finish the spoons, lightly sand them and use olive or walnut oil ④. Another technique using the pole lathe involves turning the handle on the lathe and the outline of the bowl before finishing the bowl by hand.

Using a small froe to split the blank.

Two spoon blanks.

The finished spoon.

THE RESURGENCE OF SPOON MAKING

Spoon carving is undergoing a renaissance in the UK and, for many people, it will be their first experience of working with green wood. Gatherings such as 'Spoonfest' (held in Derbyshire) bring together would-be whittlers with workshops and instruction from some of the most experienced spoon makers amidst a relaxed festival atmosphere. Meanwhile, 'Barn the Spoon' (Barn Carder) has managed to set up as a spoon maker in Hackney Road, London, where he can be found behind the glass frontage whittling spoons as the world rushes by (see page 14).

A selection of spoons by greenwood craftsman Richard Ely. Spoons in the centre have turned handles and bowls.

TO MAKE A
FREE-FORM SPOON

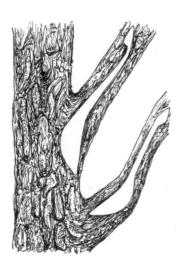

① Seeing the spoons in the trees.

Making spoons without using the pole lathe allows the whittler a freedom to go with the spoon as it evolves. This results in a varied selection of shapes of handles and bowls. It is important to look at the grain pattern within the wood before beginning carving, seeing the spoon within the tree. A curved branch will allow for the bowl and handle of the spoon while going with the grain and keeping the strength integral to the spoon ①. It is possible to make spoons with narrower handles this way as the neck of the spoon will be stronger than a turned spoon. Another approach is to mark the profile on the wood before you start whittling. Both face and edge profiles can be marked ②, ③. Another approach for roughing out the spoon bowl is to clamp the wood and gouge out the bowl before cutting out the blank. The spoon can then be finished with hand tools ④.

Split the log in two using a froe and then rough out the blank using a side axe ⑤. Stop cuts can be made with a saw to make sure you do not cut away the material saved for the bowl when you are chopping out surplus wood. Once you have a roughed-out blank, you can either draw the profile of the spoon onto the blank or just go with your intuition – you may end up with a spoon you could never have drawn!

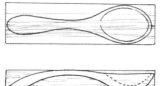

② Marking face and edge profiles before roughing out.

③ Marking out of a scoop.

④ Clamping the wood and carving out the bowl first.

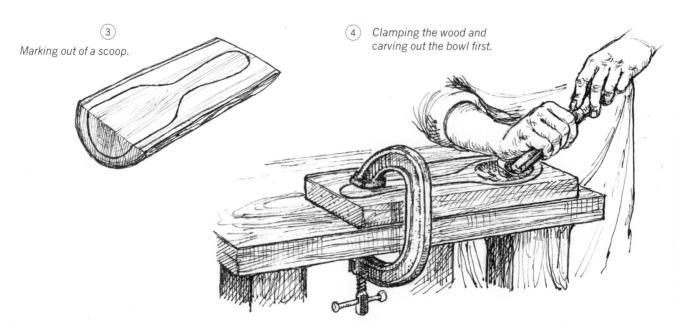

Roughing out the blank for the spoon.

From log to spoon, the four stages of free-form spoon making.

I have a spoon-whittling pouch that contains a gouge, carving knife, hooked knife (right handed) and minijarn gouge ⑥. I use the carving knife to shape the handle and outside of the bowl and the hooked knife to work on the inside. These come in right- or left-handed versions and a double-sided version, although I am not keen on this as I like to press with my thumb on the opposite side of the hooked knife to the edge. I also use a minijarn gouge. This is made by the Swedish blacksmith Hans Karlsson and, like all of his tools, is of the finest quality. The gouge allows you to curve deep into the spoon bowl. Finish by careful gouging (this takes practice) or by sanding, working up to a very fine sandpaper or else the spoon will have a 'fluffed' finish. Finally apply a food-based oil like walnut.

My whittling pouch containing (left to right) small gouge, carving knife, right-handed hook knife and minijarn gouge.

Finished free-form spoon with other half of the log (Norway maple).

A selection of spoons by Martin Hazell. Martin specializes in whittling spoons from burrs.

Domestic crafts **143**

TROUGH

This is a traditional Swedish style of trough with many different uses, whether it be as a storage container, used in bread making or catching pig blood. The detail of definition and finish is down to your own preference. Some are beautifully decorated with frieze carving, while others are simple carved logs that perform traditional household functions.

Materials you will need

One log: cut to the length of your required trough; I went for 16in (406mm) and about 7in (178mm) in diameter. This should make two troughs. Any carving wood is suitable: lime, cherry, sycamore, birch or maple. I chose a piece of Norway maple that had blown down in a neighbouring wood.
Walnut oil

Recommended tools

Shaving horse, clamps, vice, froe, side axe, draw knife, heavy framing gouge, hand gouges, dog-leg gouge, convex spokeshave, carving adze, chainsaw carving disc, sandpaper.

Splitting the log in two with a froe.

Shaping the face with a side axe.

Shaping the trough

Split the log into two using a froe ①and then start to shape the face of the log with a side axe ②. This face will be the top of the trough. Continuing with the side axe, rough out the shape of the trough by chopping the curve of the log to your chosen shape. Use a draw knife to work the shape of the trough in more detail. Clamping a trough at this stage is relatively easy as it is a solid block ③, ④, but it becomes more difficult when the bowl needs hollowing. I have settled for a combination of techniques at different stages, culminating in the use of large clamps to hold the trough to a suitable work surface. Another method is a Swedish idea courtesy of Gert Ljungberg, which keeps the trough clear of metalwork when using an adze ⑤.

Clamping the trough in a portable vice while working with a draw knife.

Using a shaving horse to grip the trough.

A Swedish design for clamping trough when hollowing with an adze.

Using a framing gouge to hollow out the trough bowl.

Hollowing the bowl

With the shape of the trough established it is time to hollow the bowl. There are many options for this. Traditionally a small carving adze would be used and is an ideal tool for the job. Use a heavy framing gouge (6) or a chainsaw carving disc to rough out the bowl. After that it is down to hand gouges and convex spokeshaves. I used the chainsaw carving disk to rough out the shape and then turned to a framing gouge to smooth off the disk marks. For a detailed finish use a dog-leg gouge (7). This beautifully designed tool is ideal for working inside bowls and troughs and soon smooths out rough edges (8). To finish the trough, sand it thoroughly for a couple of hours (9) and then apply a coat of walnut oil.

A dog-leg gouge.

Using the dog-leg gouge to smooth out the chisel marks.

The trough after sanding.

The finished trough in use.

A selection of small troughs and bowls carved by Martin Hazell.

A dog-leg gouge helps to give a detailed finish on the hollowed-out bowl of a trough.

BAR STOOL

These bar stools are a timeless design used in a traditional manner, as their name suggests. This is an all-rounder, an adaptable stool. The detail in this project is for a full-sized bar stool but it can also be made to a specific height for a specific purpose.

Materials you will need
1 round log for the legs: 30in (76cm) long x 6in (150mm) diameter
1 round log for the stretchers: 34in (86cm) long x 4in (100mm) diameter
1 air-dried plank for the seat: 14 x 14in (35.5 x 35.5cm) x 2in (50mm) thick
Ash is an excellent choice for all parts. I used sweet chestnut as it is what I had available.
Danish oil

Recommended tools
Bow saw, draw knife, spokeshave, froe, side axe, concave spokeshave, tenon cutter or hollow shoulder plane, rounding plane, protractor, sliding bevel, compass, spirit level, shaving horse, cleaving brake, jigsaw, cordless drill, maul, auger bits.

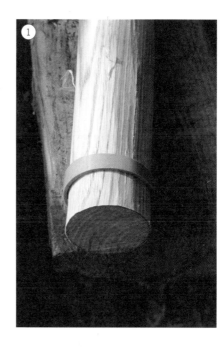

Tip
for stool making

When choosing the wood for the legs and
stretchers, I choose fresh greenwood for the legs
and a piece of the previous year's cut roundwood
for the stretchers, so that the legs will shrink
more and tighten onto the stretchers. If you
don't have the luxury of access to different ages
of wood, then make the stretchers first and dry
them for a week or two in a greenhouse or near
a stove and you will create the same result.

*Using the 2in
(50mm) pipe
round to keep an
even size down
the leg.*

The legs

First take the 30in (76cm) log, which should be green, and
quarter it using a froe and cleaving brake (see Ladder-back
chair, page 179, picture 7). Then work each quarter down to
a rough circular shape using a side axe. Working on a shaving
horse (see page 202), using a 2in (50mm) pipe round as a
guide (1), work the legs into a circle using first a draw knife
(2) and then a spokeshave. A concave spokeshave can be
a useful addition, but is not essential.

The stretchers

Take the 34in (86cm) length, saw it in half then split it out
so you have eight quartered parts (you will only need six of
them). Using a 1¼in (32mm) pipe round as a guide, follow
the same procedure as for the legs.

*Working the leg on
a shaving horse
with a draw knife.*

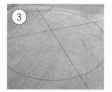

Marking out the seat for drilling the leg mortises.

Cutting out the seat shape with a jigsaw.

Using a sliding bevel to align the drill to the correct angle for drilling the leg mortises.

The leg mortises drilled.

Measuring the centres to ensure the distance between the legs is even.

The seat

Next take the 2in (50mm)-thick air-dried plank and, using a compass, draw a circle with a 6½in (165mm) radius. This will be the outside of your stool seat. Draw another circle with a radius of 5⅝in (143mm) and draw two lines bisecting the circle at right angles to each other ③. Where the lines bisect the inner circle will be the centre of the mortises for the legs. Cut out the seat using a jigsaw ④.

The legs should be drilled at 12 degrees off vertical to allow them to splay outwards for stability. With the protractor at 102 degrees, set the sliding bevel to the angle and offer the bevel up whilst you drill the mortises. If working on your own, make up an angle block set at 102 degrees (see Ladder-back chair, page 184, picture 36). This way you do not need an extra person to hold the sliding bevel in position while you eye the angle when you drill. I drilled the mortises to 1½in (38mm) deep. Put red tape on the auger bit to ensure you don't drill too far ⑤, ⑥.

There are a number of options here. I decided not to drill right through the seat as I did not want to wedge the ends of the legs in case the air-dried sweet chestnut split. I used some glue in the mortise as the legs will shrink and the attachment to the seat could become loose. If you want to avoid using glue then, once you have fitted the stretchers to the legs, allow the legs to shrink-dry before fitting them to the seat.

Or, choose a seat from a wood less prone to split and drill right through the seat. Wedge the ends of the legs, ensuring that the wedge is hammered in at a right angle to the grain of the wood in the seat.

⑧ *Dimensions for the stool.*

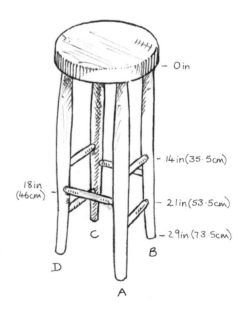

Assembling the stool

Using a 1in (25mm) rounding plane, taper the ends of the legs and, using a maul, tap the legs into the mortises in the inverted seat. Measure the distances between the legs and adjust by twisting them to get the distance even (7). Check the diagonal measurements between the legs as well to check they are in square. Label each leg and its corresponding mortise to be sure to replace them as you have them now after the stretchers are fitted. I use the labels A, B, C and D. Measuring from the inside of the upturned seat, mark the stretcher positions at 14in (355mm) and 21in (533mm) between legs A and B and between legs C and D (8). Check the marks are level and extend the level lines on the legs as this will give you the angle to drill the mortises. Measure the internal distances between the legs at these points and add on 2in (50mm) as each stretcher will go 1in (25mm) into each leg.

Remove the legs and drill mortise holes 1in (25mm) deep with a 5/8in (16mm) drill bit. Take the stretchers and cut them to the internal distances, plus 2in (50mm). Using a 5/8in (16mm) tenon cutter, or a hollow shoulder plane, cut 1in (25mm) tenons on each end of the stretchers. I put the stretchers in a vice and check they are level then, using a cordless drill and tenon cutter, checking the bubble is also level on the tenon cutter, cut the tenons (9). Now fit the two stretchers between legs A and B and legs C and D and stand pairs of legs in the seat mortises (10). Re-check the legs are all in square and, measuring up from the inside of the upturned seat again, measure 18in (457mm) and mark level lines on the legs between legs A and C and B and D. Again, measure internal distances and add on 2in (50mm). Repeat the process of drilling the legs and cutting the tenons on the stretchers then join all four legs (11).

Tap all four legs as one unit into the upturned seat mortises. Once you are happy you have a good fit and the legs are even, place a little glue in the seat mortises and firmly fix the legs in place for the final time. Stand the stool on a level floor and position a spirit level on the seat. Chock any of the legs with cardboard (12) to ensure the seat is perfectly level and then, using a small block of wood and a pencil, draw around all four legs (13). Cut the legs to the pencil lines and your stool will be level. Sand the legs and stool seat and finish with your chosen oil: I used Danish oil.

Using a 5/8in (16mm) tenon cutter for the stretcher tenons.

Legs A and B and legs C and D with stretchers fitted.

Fitting the single stretchers between the four legs.

Marking each leg prior to cutting the legs level.

Levelling the legs.

The finished bar stool.

Enjoying a pint at the bar. The seats on the three stools are sweet chestnut (nearest and furthest) and wych elm (centre).

WALKING STICKS

Walking sticks can be made from most woods. Many a country stick is chosen for its unusual character – be it the corkscrew twist that appears when honeysuckle entwines itself with woods such as hazel or ash, or a sturdy root stick made from blackthorn (my favourite type). Thumb sticks are made from the forking pattern where the main stem divides into two.

SOURCING STICKS

As some of my winter work involves laying hedges, I am in a good position to collect sticks suitable for making walking sticks. Hedgerows are often a good source of hawthorn and blackthorn sticks. Having laid the hedge, it is worth returning a few years later as by then many upright stems will have grown from the near horizontally laid hedging material and the handle and stem are already set at a right angle. In Sussex, in the surrounding chestnut coppices where I live, some sweet chestnut is still cut on a three-year rotation purely for walking sticks. These sticks all go to the National Health Service, so if you are unfortunate enough to end up in hospital in England for a sprained ankle or knee, have a good look at the stick you are given: it will be a steam-bent sweet chestnut stick.

To make a
STEAM-BENT WALKING STICK

Materials you will need

1 straight stick of ash, hazel or sweet chestnut: 4ft (1.2m) long x 1¼ (32mm) diameter (the sizing of a stick varies from person to person, so it is best to make a longer stick and then cut to the required length later)

A ferrule (this can be pre-bought or made from a piece of copper pipe or the end of a used shotgun cartridge)

Linseed oil

Recommended tools

Pruning saw, spokeshave, bending jig, steam-bending equipment, sandpaper.

Choose a knot-free stick and cut a notch into it 1in (25mm) from the end. The stick can now be steamed. This can either be done by using a steamer ① as described in previous projects (see page 182), or, where a number of sticks are being made, it is common to place the end of the stick (with the notch) in damp sand, heated over a stove. After steaming, place the stick into a bending jig consisting of a round wooden wheel of around 5in (125mm) diameter. The ones I use are turned from oak and a 1in (25mm) peg ②.

Place the steamed stick between the wheel and the peg with the notch facing away from the wheel and push through beyond the wheel as this will be cut off when the stick is finished. Rotate the handle clockwise about 200 degrees. Overbend the handle to allow for some movement back later when the stick is released. Tie a loop of twine around the notch and the handle to hold the stick in position and leave it to cool and set ③.

When set, remove the cord and the handle will spring back into its finished position. To finish the stick, sand and oil with linseed. Many sticks are left with the bark on as this is part of the rustic character ④ but if you prefer to finish the stick without the bark, or if the bark has begun to come away after steaming, now is the time to clean up the stick with a spokeshave. A stick is usually left long and then cut to the size of the user. Once the length is established a ferrule can be fitted on the end of the stick ⑤. This will protect the end against the impact of the ground. It is useful to have a variety of sizes of ferrule available to choose one slightly smaller than the end diameter of the stick. Pare down the end of the stick to fit and tap on the ferrule with a hammer. Then, using a blunt nail, hammer three indents into the side of the ferrule at equidistant intervals to secure it in place.

Sticks in a steamer, awaiting steam.

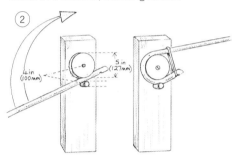

The stick-bending jig.

A steam-bent chestnut stick.

The finished bent stick handle.

The fitted ferrule.

To make a
CROSS-HEAD WALKING STICK

stage 1

Choose a young sapling.

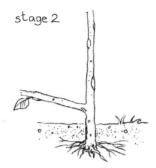

stage 2

Remove the side branches except the lowest one.

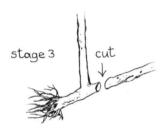

stage 3   cut

Lift from the ground and cut off the lead stem just above the side branch.

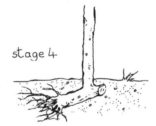

stage 4

Replant with the remains of the original main stem horizontal underground

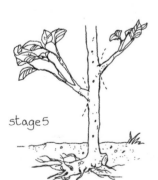

stage 5

Prune off any large side branches. Allow the main stem to grow to about 1¼in (32cm) diameter.

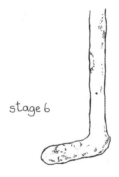

stage 6

Dig up and clean off the roots. Trim back for a natural grown handle.

The process of growing a cross-head stick.

Another type of walking stick is the cross-head stick. There are two ways to make them. One is to find it growing and involves digging out part of the root (I obtained my favourite blackthorn stick this way). The other is by pruning and replanting a young sapling, which is common with ash. This is a method that requires patience as you are growing your stick. However, growing a natural handle takes only a few years and, once underway, a few saplings can be planted each year. You will soon have a good supply of naturally grown handles. The handles are always of interest but it is the strength of these sticks that gives them such longevity. The grain of the wood flows through unchecked from the handle to the stick. I have an old ash cross-head stick that belonged to my grandfather. This must be about 40 years of age and is still in good shape.

The head of my favourite blackthorn stick.

My grandfather's cross-head stick.

CHERRY-PICKING
BASKET

Baskets come in a variety of sizes and shapes. Their lightweight form makes them a particularly useful type of container to have to hand. Over time, the diverse weaving techniques of basketry have spread out to encompass a wide range of products from furniture to fish traps, from hats through to coffins. The amazing versatility of a flexible plant-based material and a pattern of weaving can produce a large array of different products. The cherry-picking basket made here is a traditional bucket-shaped basket that is hardwearing and strong.

MEET THE MAKER

Martin Hazell

Martin Hazell, a renowned basket and spoon maker, paid me a visit at Prickly Nut Wood to share his knowledge about basket making. Martin was working for the Wildlife Trust in Shropshire in the 1990s when he visited an old colleague who was making baskets. Inspired by the rhythmic patterns and repetition, he started making a few himself. The making of baskets soon became an obsession that was more important than his regular job – so he made it his regular job. Martin then trained with basket maker Jenny Crisp, who helped him refine his technique. Since then he has taught basket making and more recently has travelled as a nomadic basket maker and spoon carver, sharing and learning different techniques in Europe.

"What I really like about basket making is taking a really unpromising bunch of sticks and then turning them into an organized and beautiful thing, making something you can use. It's empowering knowing you can make stuff, you don't need to just buy it and the pleasure of making it is a boost to the spirit."

Martin Hazell with one of his baskets.

Materials you will need
Approximately 125 pre-soaked willow rods: 5ft (1.5m) long
This project uses two varieties of willow: 'Whissender', a form of *Salix triandra* for the base and uprights; and 'Norbury', a form of *Salix purpurea* for the weave.

Recommended tools
Bodkin, rapping iron, knife, secateurs. (Martin, travelling light, used a pair of electrical side snips for trimming up the willow, a pocket knife and a carved piece of wood for the bodkin.)

13in (330mm)

8in (200mm)

8½in (216mm)

9in (225mm)

Dimensions of the cherry-picking basket.

Beds of willow ready for harvesting.

TYPES OF BASKET

Baskets in England are woven primarily with willow and much of the industry is based around the osier beds of the Somerset levels. That being said, there is a growing interest in hedgerow baskets, with materials like bramble, dogwood and honeysuckle being used to create beautiful baskets. More solid baskets are made from thinly split wood like Devon splint baskets and the Sussex trug. These are hardwearing and popular. The Sussex trug is an institution amongst gardeners and there is a steady trade for the trug makers of Herstmonceaux, who make their trugs from sweet chestnut and willow.

An unusual chestnut basket/box from the Weald and Downland museum.

Birch bark and willow makes an attractive combination.

The Sussex trug.

Selection of willow baskets at a fair.

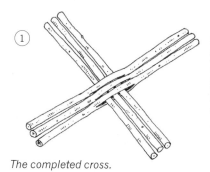

① The completed cross.

② Opening the willow in the centre, to insert the other sticks to form the cross.

③ Beginning pairing.

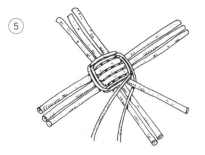

④ Ready to open up the sticks to form a wheel.

⑤ Opening out the sticks to form a wheel.

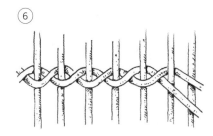

⑥ Pairing.

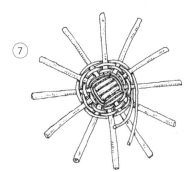

⑦ Continued pairing around the wheel.

⑧ Continued pairing to form the base.

⑨ The completed base.

Soaking the willow

Pre-soak the willow in water for four days. The general rule is one day per 1ft (30cm). This process can be sped up by using warm water. Once the willow has been soaked, it needs to be used within a few days.

The base

Choose six fairly robust rods and cut to about 8in (200mm) long to form the slath (the round base). Split three of them in the centre section of the rod and insert the other three rods through them ①. The usual tool for this job is a bodkin (a steel spike with a handle). However, Martin whittled a pointed piece of wood, which he pushed through the willow in place of a bodkin ②. Begin pairing (the most-used balanced weave) by placing two more rods to one side of the three rods that have passed through the three split willow rods. Weave one rod under three then over three and the other rod over three and under three ③. Do two rounds in this way ④ and then open up the cross into a wheel shape ⑤.

Pull down on the wheel rods to create a dished shape like the base of a champagne bottle. This will be stronger and the weave will tighten as downward pressure is applied on the base of the basket. Continue pairing by weaving over one then under one ⑥ around the whole wheel ⑦, ⑧. Finish the base by tucking the tip ends into the last row of weaving. The base is now complete ⑨. Martin makes a number of bases and leaves them for a few days to dry out while he selects and grades material and then stakes up and weaves a number of baskets at the same time.

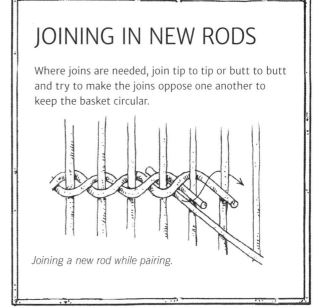

Getting the angle of the knife correct for slyping.

The finished slype.

JOINING IN NEW RODS

Where joins are needed, join tip to tip or butt to butt and try to make the joins oppose one another to keep the basket circular.

Joining a new rod while pairing.

Rods slyped and ready to insert into the base.

Inserting the uprights into the base.

Staking up

Look for 24 rods for the uprights. When you look closely at them you will see that they have all grown with a slight curve and this can be used to help shape the finished basket. Use the rods with the convex side of the curve leaning outwards. Using a sharp knife make a slype (a slanted cut) at the butt end of each rod ⑩, ⑪, ⑫. Push the uprights carefully into the base a couple of inches deep, with the slyped end going in first and without bending them. There should be one on each side of the 12 spokes of the wheel that form the base ⑬, ⑭. Once they are all in place, apply pressure with the back of a knife and bend each rod upwards ⑮. Then tie all the rods together ⑯ to keep them at the correct angle to start working the upsett.

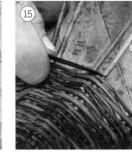

Using the back of the knife to put pressure on the rod where it will bend upwards.

Hooped and tied rods.

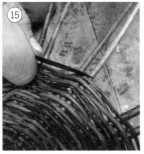

The base with the uprights inserted.

Inserting rods to begin weaving the upsett.

Three-rod wale, inserting the weavers.

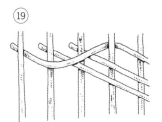

Starting with the left-hand rod, weave 'in front of two, behind one'.

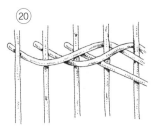

Weaving the second rod, weave 'in front of two, behind one'.

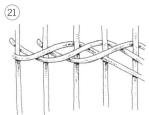

Weaving the third rod, weave 'in front of two, behind one'.

Martin randing the upsett.

The upsett

This is the first 1–1¹/₂in (25–38mm) of the side of the basket. The key role of the upsett is to separate the stakes evenly and to set them at the correct angle for the remainder of the basket weave. Martin chose a four-rod, pull-down wale weave. Waling is a strong weave and ideally suited for the upsett, where control is needed to keep the stakes in place. The pull-down wale does as its name suggests and ensures the rods are pulled down as the wale pattern is weaved.

Begin with eight rods and insert four of them in two pairs on either side of two of the wheel spokes ⑰. Weave one rod at a time in between the uprights 'in front of two, behind one', pulling down to fill in the gap between the uprights and the base. Next insert four rods opposite the first four and weave the same pattern in the same direction. When the first rod meets the position where you started weaving, cut it off. The weave pattern now becomes a three-rod wale ⑱, ⑲, ⑳, ㉑. Work two sets at the same time for evenness of the basket, continuing the weave 'in front of two, behind one'. The three-rod wale is a very useful weave for keeping the basket nice and even. Where these two sets run out insert two more sets of three rods by inserting them at the midpoints between where you began the previous two sets. Continue weaving the three-rod wale until the upsett is approximately 1–2in (25–50mm).

Use an axe handle to rand the weave. Randing is the process of rapping down the weave to keep it tight and even. This would usually be usually done with a randing iron but Martin shows the versatility of how few tools you need in basket making by using the handle of a tool ㉒.

WALING

This is a strong type of weave and is often used to strengthen a basket when changing from one weave to another. A three-rod wale uses three rods, a four-rod wale uses four rods, etc. The pattern can vary, for example, a four-rod wale could also be 'in front of two, behind two'.

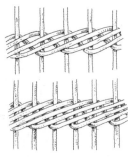

Example of a four-rod wale, weave 'in front of three, behind one'.

Example of a five-rod wale, weave 'in front of four, behind one'.

The main weave

Continue the weave by using a 'double French rand' ㉓. Randing (when referring to a weave) is a term that describes the pattern 'in front of one rod, behind one rod'. A double rand refers to two rods worked in pairs, weaving 'in front of one, behind one'. Weave 'in front of one, behind one' once with one pair and then move onto the next pair, and so on in an anticlockwise direction. This weave looks complicated as there are many rods attached to the basket at one time, but it is simpler than it looks and the double rand ensures fast progress up the sides.

Select and slype 24 even-sized rods and insert them into the weave behind each upright to become the lower set ㉔. Select another 24 rods, slightly thinner than the lower set. Slype and then insert them into the weave directly above the lower ones to become the upper set ㉕. There are now 48 rods to weave in total, in 24 pairs. Weave 'in front of one, behind one' with the pairs of rods ㉖ and rap down the weave every couple of rows. ㉗, ㉘, ㉙.

When the weave reaches the desired height, return to the three-rod wale to consolidate the rand underneath ㉚. Choose 12 rods and begin with three rods opposite each other then butt joint the other six rods in and continue the three-rod wale to a similar depth as the upsett. At this point, put in spacers for the handle (see picture 35 overleaf) and weave the three-rod wale around them. These will leave a gap when they are removed and facilitate the fitting of the handle. Martin chooses to align the handle with the original rods that form one part of the cross in the base of the basket.

Detail of the double French rand weave.

Inserting the lower set of 24 rods for the beginning of the double French rand.

Inserting the upper set of 24 rods for weaving the double French rand.

Weaving in pairs, the double French rand, 'in front of one, behind one'.

Notice the thumb position, keeping the upright rods in the correct position while weaving around them.

Looking down on the basket. Martin's attention to keeping the shape is clearly visible.

The sides going up.

The three-rod wale above the double French rand consolidates the weave and strengthens the basket top.

SLEWING

Another fast weave that is great for using up offcuts, different sized pieces of willow and other materials is slewing. This could be used as an alternative to the double French rand. A two-rod slew would mean weaving around the basket in pairs 'in front of one, behind one'. When one tip gets too narrow, add another rod above the existing pair and weave with this new pair. Continue in this way until the desired height is reached. This works best with an uneven number of uprights, but it is possible to slew with an even number if you start with the two rods on opposite sides of the basket. Once you have woven the length of half a rod, add in the second. Slewing uses up odd length rods and avoids having 48 rods to deal with at one time.

(31) *Example of trac border, 'in front of two, behind one'.*

Bending over the five rods that go behind two.

Taking the first rod that was bent over 'in front of four, behind one'. (Note the three uprights together in the picture are actually one upright and the two handle spacers and therefore count as one).

Bending the next upright 'behind two, over the top of the one that you have just taken in front of four, behind one'.

The finished border with handle spacers.

The bow rods fitted to the basket.

Wrapping the rods around the bow rods.

Taking the ends of the twisted rods through the wale weave.

Bringing each rod around the handle and back through the wale weave.

All the rods tied in.

Trimming off the excess willow.

Looking into the finished basket.

The finished basket.

The top border

There are many different styles of border depending on the finished look and use of the basket. A trac border ③① is one of the simplest styles but Martin chose a patterned border, as follows. Take five existing rods and bend each one against your thumbnail about ½in (1cm) up from the top of the wale beneath. Twist each rod and lay it behind two uprights ③②. The first rod that was bent over now goes 'in front of four uprights, behind one' ③③. The sixth upright is bent over and goes 'behind two, over the top of the first rod' ③④. This pattern is continued to complete the border to a width of about 1in (25mm) or more if you prefer a wider border and the tips are tucked in to finish ③⑤.

The handle

This basket has a wrapped handle but you could also have a twisted or rope handle (see box opposite). For the wrapped handle, pick a pair of rods for the bow and pre-bend them over your knee to avoid them kinking. Remove the handle spacers, slype both ends of the rods and push them firmly into position where the spacers were ③⑥. Select ten long, slender rods. (You will need at least eight, but possibly nine or ten.) Insert two rods each side of the bow rods and wrap three times around the bow rods, being careful to make sure the two rods stay aligned next to one another and don't cross over ③⑦. Then repeat from the opposite side. If there is a gap in the bow, add another rod or two to fill in. Using a bodkin (or whittled spike) open a gap through the wale weave below the border and pull the rods through ③⑧. Then take each rod individually around the handle, pulling tight and then threaded back through the wale being careful to ensure they don't twist over each other ③⑨, ④⓪. Repeat on the opposite side. Trim off any excess willow with side snips ④① and your basket is complete ④②, ④③.

TWISTED OR ROPE HANDLES

This type of handle is commonly used on large baskets such as log baskets. Select four 5ft (1.5m)-long rods. Slype one end of the first rod and insert it where the handle spacers have been removed. Make a suitable curve for the handle and then pass the other end from the inside of the basket through the wale and out the other side ①. Twist a second rod to separate the fibres (as if making cordage ②) and push one end into the border at the opposite end of the handle curve to where the first rod was inserted. Twist three times around the first rod. Then go through the wale and out the other side and weave back around the first rod and then through the wale. Now take up the end of the first rod and wrap that around the handle. Go through the wale and weave both ends into the wale weave ③.

Martin twisting the willow to separate the fibres and make it behave more like cordage.

The first rod inserted to form the handle bow.

The finished twisted handle.

BENTWOOD CHAIR

Chair making is a detailed craft that can require patience, as shown with the ladder-back rocking chair (see page 176). However, most people begin with simple rustic versions such as slab chairs and stick chairs before moving on to the more complex types. One of the main differences is that the rustic stick chair is usually made from wood in the round that hasn't been quartered prior to construction. These chairs can be quick to make and some will last well. Bentwood chairs take the rustic stick frame and add curves made of woods such as willow and hazel. These chairs are attractive, easy to make and can be surprisingly comfortable.

Materials you will need

I mainly use sweet chestnut for the frame and hazel for the bentwood. In the UK, hazel and willow are the favoured species, while in the US willow is the dominant species used, with occasional chairs being made from alder or cottonwood.

For the frame

13 sticks for the stretchers: 24in (60cm) long x 1¹/₂in (38mm) diameter
2 sticks for the front legs: 16in (40.5cm) long x 2in (50mm) diameter
2 sticks for the back legs: 30in (76cm) long x 2in (50mm) diameter
1 stick for the top bar: 3ft (90cm) long x 2in (50mm) diameter
2 sticks for the diagonal braces: 25¹/₂in (65cm) long x 1¹/₂in (38mm) diameter

Bentwood

3 rods for the bow back: 10ft (3.05m) long x ⁵/₈in (16mm) diameter
6 rods for the arms: 5ft 6in (1.7m) long ⁵/₈in (16mm) diameter
13 rods for the seat/back rods: 5ft (1.5m) long x ⁵/₈in (16mm) diameter
Silicon bronze ring-shank nails: 1³/₁₆in (30mm) and 1¹/₂in (38mm)
Galvanized nails: 3in (75mm)
Danish oil

Recommended tools

Bow saw, cordless drill, small hammer, secateurs, spirit level, protractor, carpenter's square.

A rustic slab chair by Richard Bates.

FIRST CHAIRS

The first rustic chair I made was for my son Rowan and two more children have enjoyed it since. It is still in fine condition, awaiting the next generation – quite an achievement considering it was made from three-year-old sweet chestnut coppice.

Paul South with his first chair. An unusual chestnut stick chair with chestnut bast back and seat.

My first chair, 20 years on.

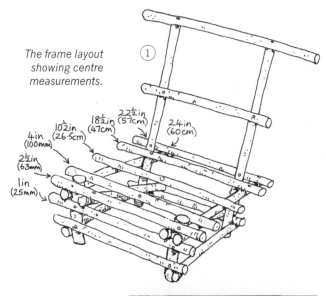

The frame layout showing centre measurements.

4in (100mm)
2½in (63mm)
1in (25mm)
10½in (26.5cm)
18½in (47cm)
22½in (57cm)
24in (60cm)

Assembling the stick frame

First, assemble the stick frame of the chair (1). Find a straight-edged piece of timber to use as a level line from which to lay out the side frames. The front legs should be straight and the back legs should be angled back at 12 degrees off vertical. The top stretcher on each side frame should be slightly angled towards the back legs whereas the lower stretcher should be level (2). Drill the side frames and nail together with 3in (75mm) galvanized nails.

Drill and nail the cross stretchers. Check with a spirit level that the sides are level with each other (3). Drill and nail diagonal braces from the front top stretcher to the back bottom stretcher (4). Drill and nail them into the legs as well as the stretchers (two-way nailing) (5). Attach seat stretchers, a top bar across the top of the back legs and another stretcher across the inside of the back legs, midway between seat stretchers and top bar, to complete the frame (6).

Adding the bentwood

Start with the bow back. I use silicon bronze ring-shank nails of 1¾₁₆in (30mm) and 1½in (38mm). These are very thin, so a ⁵⁄₆₄in (2mm) drill bit is ideal for pre-drilling. Fix one end to the inside of the lower stretcher of the side frame where it meets the back leg and bring it around in a curve so that it will attach to the back of the top bar. This first piece must attach to the top bar, leaving room outside of it to attach the other two parts of the bow back (7). Work the bentwood in your hands to even out the bow. Spend some time getting the first bow looking good as the others will follow its shape and the look of the chair is often defined by this curve. When satisfied with the shape, fix to both sides of the top bar with 1½in (38mm) silicon bronze nails and fix the end to the inside of the opposing lower side frame stretcher. Next, fix the second bow back rod to the lower side frame stretcher against the first bow-back rod. As the second bow-back rod twists around and follows the profile of the first, drill and nail it to the first bow-back rod at approximately every 8in (200mm). Repeat this process for the third bow-back rod (8).

Laying out the side frames using a straight-edged piece of timber to level from.

Using a level to check the frame.

Diagonal braces create stability in the frame.

Two-way nailing of the diagonal brace. This helps make the frame rigid.

The frame once it is completed.

Beginning the bow back.

The completed bow back.

First rods for the arms.

Attach the arms to the inside of the front lower cross stretcher. Position the first arm rod approximately 6in (150mm) from the centre of the front leg and then bend it so that it attaches to the front upper cross stretcher, curves around and is fixed to the top bar inside of the bow back. Again, work the bentwood to ensure the curve is both aesthetically pleasing and comfortable for the user's arms. Match the curve of the first arm with the opposing arm on the other side of the chair ⑨. Getting a good match with the arms is important for the balance and aesthetics of the chair. Attach the second arm rod to the inside of the lower cross stretcher next to the first arm rod. Twist it around the first arm rod before finishing on the bow-back side of the first arm on the top bar. Fix the second arm rod to the first arm rod at approximately 8in (200mm) intervals in the same way that you fixed the bow-back rods. Fit the second arm rod to the opposing arm and then follow the same pattern with the third arm rods ⑩.

The last part is to infill the seat and back. The pattern for this infill can take many forms, which is part of the beauty of this bentwood technique. At this stage you can let your imagination dictate the pattern. I chose a pattern that brings the seat rods in at the centre of the back and then opens out again as it meets the bow back ⑪.

Start with the centre rod and then work out the spacing to keep the infill of rods even on each side. Tuck the rods under the front upper cross stretcher and then fix them to the second seat cross stretcher and to where the seat rods curve upwards. Fix the rods to the middle back stretcher and then take the top of the rods behind the bow back. Fix the top of the rods to the back of the bow-back curve. Drill and fix into the back of the lower bow-back rod and then cut off the surplus with secateurs, so that the seat rods do not disturb the view of the bow back when looked at from the front. Drill and fix the seat rod through the middle bow-back rod as well, so they are double fixed.

Finish the chair with Danish oil. These types of chairs need to be kept inside during bad weather if they are to give you a few good years of use.

The arms completed – note the way each rod twists over the previous one, from front to back of the chair.

The completed chair.

Tip
for bending rods

The process of bending the rods from the seat to the back should be done slowly as there is a chance the fibres could break.

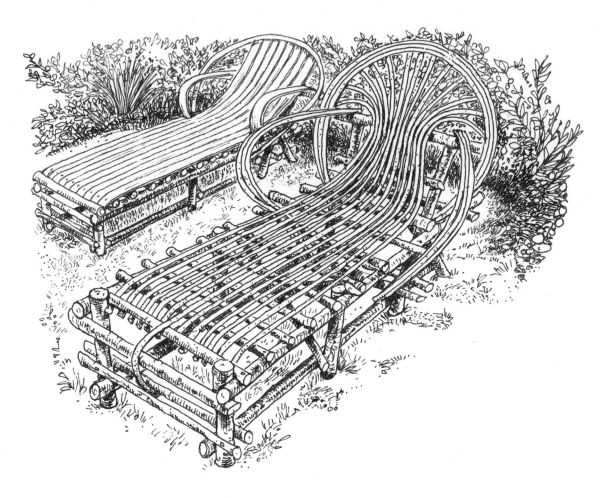

BENTWOOD AND STEAM-BENT
LOUNGERS

The structure of these loungers is similar to the bentwood chair on page 164. Here, I have extended the frame to allow for longer rods of hazel to create the lounger. I have gone for a similar pattern in the back of the bentwood lounger to create a two-part set with the chair but the design of the back is down to your own imagination. The steam-bent lounger is an adaptation of the bentwood lounger. It is more classic in style and, as it is made from sweet chestnut which is very durable, it will last longer than the bentwood lounger.

To make a
BENTWOOD LOUNGER

Materials you will need

I mainly use sweet chestnut for the frame and hazel for the bentwood. In the UK, hazel and willow are the favoured species, while in the US willow is the dominant species used, with occasional chairs being made from alder or cottonwood.

For the frame

4 sticks for the side-frame stretchers:
5ft 10in (1.78m) long x 2in (50mm) diameter
4 sticks for the front and middle legs:
14in (35.5cm) long x 2in (50mm) diameter
2 sticks for the rear legs: 26in (66cm) long x 2in (50mm) diameter
14 sticks for the cross stretchers: 26in (66cm) long x 1¹/₂in (38mm) diameter
1 stick for the arm cross stretcher: 32in (81cm) long x 1¹/₂in (38mm) diameter
1 stick for the top bar: 3ft 1in (94cm) long x 1¹/₂in (38mm) diameter
1 stick for the cross stretcher on seat: 26in (66cm) x long 2¹/₂in (63mm) diameter
2 sticks for the diagonal cross braces: 27in (68.6cm) long x 1¹/₂in (38mm) diameter
2 sticks for the diagonal back braces: 15in (38cm) long x 1¹/₄in (31mm) diameter
2 sticks for the rear leg struts: 18in (46cm) x 1¹/₄in (31mm) diameter

Bentwood

3 rods for the bow back: 10ft (3.05m) long x ⁵/₈in (16mm) diameter
6 rods for the arms: 5ft 6in (1.68m) x ⁵/₈in (16mm) diameter
13 rods for the seat: 8ft (2.4m) x ⁵/₈in (16mm) diameter
Silicon bronze ring-shank nails: 1³/₁₆in (30mm) and 1¹/₂in (38mm)
Galvanized ring shanks: 3in (75mm)
Danish oil

Recommended tools

Bow saw, cordless drill, small hammer, secateurs, spirit level, protractor, carpenter's square.

Assembling the stick frame

This project begins by laying out two side frames on the workshop floor. I use the line of a straight floor board as a guide level and lay out the legs and top and bottom stretchers. Note that the top and bottom stretchers are on opposing sides of the legs. Place a spare piece wood of a similar diameter under the legs to keep them level. Drill and nail the top stretcher and then the bottom stretcher. The rear legs are angled at 22 degrees off vertical ①, ②. When making up the second side frame be careful to ensure you make a mirror image of the first, not a copy. Stand up the two side frames (they should stand up on their own on a level floor) and check with a spirit level that they are level across the seat ③.

① *Measurements for the positions of timber for the lounger frame.*

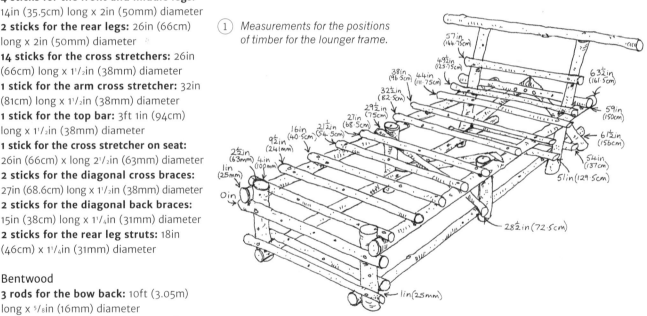

The side frame of the lounger completed. Note the bottom stretcher is to the inside of the legs while the top stretcher is to the outside.

The side frame stood up.

Cross bracing in the centre of the lounger.

Rear view of the lounger showing bracing and supports.

The completed lounger frame.

The bow back fixed to the lounger.

Detail of the fixing position for the bow back and arm rods.

Add the 14 cross stretchers (as shown in drawing 1) by drilling and nailing. Attach the diagonal cross braces from the lower side-frame stretcher on one side to the upper side-frame stretcher on the opposing side, where they meet the middle legs ④. Use two-way nailing for strength (see also page 166). The next stage is to add the rear leg struts and rear diagonal bracing. Attach the leg struts to the outside of the lower side-frame stretchers, behind the rear legs. Angle the leg struts so that they support the rear legs just below the rear seat cross stretcher. Then attach rear diagonal braces from the outside of the lower side-frame stretchers to meet with an angled cut in the centre of the rear seat cross stretcher ⑤. The frame should now be complete and ready for adding the bentwood ⑥.

Attaching the bentwood

If possible, choose straight rods with a minimum amount of taper and of even diameter. The rods can be worked between your hands to loosen the fibres and help shape them. Attach one end of the first rod to the inside of the lower side-frame stretcher up against the lower cross stretcher, behind the rear legs. Bend the rod around the outside of the upper side-frame stretcher, curve to attach it to the top bar and then to the opposing side of the top bar. Continue the curve down again to attach to the inside of the opposing lower side-frame stretcher to the one you first fixed it to. Make sure the bow looks pleasing as the next two rods will follow the same curve. Attach the second rod next to the first and, as the rod twists around and follows the profile of the first one, drill and nail it to the first rod at approximately every 8in (200mm). Repeat the process for the third bow-back rod ⑦.

Attach the arms to the inside of the lower side-frame stretcher just in front of the lower cross stretcher in front of the rear legs ⑧. Bend the rod around the outside of the upper side-frame stretcher then curve it and fix it to the top bar inside of the bow back. Again, work the hazel to ensure the curve is both aesthetically pleasing and comfortable for the user's arms. Match the curve of the first arm with the opposing arm on the other side of the lounger. Getting a good match with the arms is important for the balance and aesthetics of the lounger. Attach the second arm rod to the inside of the lower cross stretcher next to the first arm rod. Twist it around the first arm rod before finishing on the bow-back side of the first arm on the top bar. Fix the second arm rod to the first arm rod at approximately 8in (200mm) intervals in the same way that you fixed the bow-back rods. Fit the second arm rod to the opposing arm and then follow the same pattern with the third arm rod ⑨.

The last job is to infill the seat and back. I chose a pattern that brings the seat rods in at the centre of the back and then opens out again as it meets the bow back, to match the bentwood chair (see page 167) ⑩. First add the larger-diameter cross stretcher on the seat to lift the hazel rods and make a comfortable curve for the lounger. To find the best position, I used a camping mat and laid it on the lounger so the position of this larger cross stretcher could be adjusted to the most comfortable place ⑪.

The arms completed.

The infill pattern on the bentwood lounger matches the bentwood chair (page 164) to make a set.

Beginning with the centre rod, work out the spacing needed to keep the infill of rods even on each side. Tuck the rods under the front upper cross stretcher and then fix them to the second seat cross stretcher and again on the remaining cross stretchers. Fix them on the middle back stretcher before finishing behind the bow back. I took the very centre rod and fixed it to the inside of the lower front cross stretcher for a bit of variation. The process of bending the hazel from the seat to the back should be done slowly as there is a chance the hazel fibres could break at this point. Fix the rods to the middle back stretcher and then take the top of the rods behind the bow back. The top of the rods are then fixed to the back of the bow-back curve. Drill and fix into the back of the lower bow-back rod and then cut off the surplus with secateurs so that the seat rods do not disturb the view of the bow back from the front. Drill and fix the seat rod through the middle bow-back rod as well, so they are double fixed into the bow back.

Finish with a coat of Danish oil to add to the longevity of the lounger. The lounger should be kept under cover in adverse weather conditions to give it a longer life.

Using the camping roll mat to check comfort and choose the position of the larger-diameter seat cross stretcher.

Tip
for rustic furniture

The given dimensions and positions of the components are just a guide. Rustic furniture encourages the maker to blur the boundaries and use their imagination, so don't hold back if you want to adapt the design.

Rear view of the completed lounger.

The finished lounger.

Bentwood lounger, steam-bent lounger, bar stools and bentwood chair displayed around the natural swimming pond at Prickly Nut Wood.

To make a
STEAM-BENT LOUNGER

Materials you will need

Use sweet chestnut or a similar durable hardwood.
This project needs the input of a mobile sawmill to mill the
sawn lath. If you do not have access to a sawmill, the lath
can be milled on a stationary bandsaw at a joiner's workshop.

For the frame

Use the same materials list as the bentwood lounger frame
on page 169

For the seat and arms

1 fairly straight-grained log for the lath: 8ft (2.4m) long
x 8in (200mm) diameter
1 pole for the bent bow back: 9ft (2.7m) long
x 1¹/₂in (38mm) diameter
**1 length (to be fixed where the sawn lath begins to bend
upwards):** 26in (66cm) long x 2¹/₂in (63mm) diameter
Natural UV protection oil

Recommended tools

Bow saw, cordless drill, small hammer, secateurs, spirit level,
protractor, carpenter's square, mobile sawmill, steam-bending
equipment, gauntlets, chainsaw carving disc, nails.

Assembling the frame

Follow exactly the same procedure as for making up the frame
for the bentwood lounger, see pages 169–170.

The bow back

Peel the 9ft (2.7m) pole and place it in the steamer for one
and a half hours. My steamer has a large narrow steam box
as I designed it for bending yurt hoops (1). The amount of
bending needed for this lounger is not great, so a marine
plywood box over a steaming cauldron with an access hole for
the steam in the base of the box would work. Or, a heavy-duty
plastic pipe and an electric wallpaper stripper to provide the
steam can be useful. Remember to take care when working
with steam and wear gauntlets to avoid burns. As my steam
box is metal I need to place a sacrificial piece of wood under
the sweet chestnut to stop the tannins in the sweet chestnut
and metal reacting. Otherwise, I would have a purple/black
piece of timber when I removed it!

Remove the chestnut pole from the steamer and bend
around the former and clamp into place. A plywood former
with clamping positions would be best, but for this project
I compromised and used blocks fixed to the workshop floor
and clamped the bow back to these. I used a piece of hazel to
bend inside the blocks to check the shape was as I wanted (2).
Leave it to go cold before removing and fixing in position on
the chestnut frame.

The chestnut bow back should be drilled and nailed to the
inside of the lower side-frame stretcher up against the lower
cross stretcher, behind the rear legs. Bend the pole around the
outside of the upper side-frame stretcher and curve to attach
to the top bar and then to the opposing side of the top bar.
Continue down again to attach to the inside of the opposing
lower side-frame stretcher to the one you first fixed it to.

*My steam-bending set-up with
an army field boiler providing
the steam.*

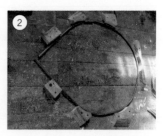

*Testing the shape of the
former with a piece of hazel.*

The lath

Mill the sweet chestnut log into ⁹/₃₂in (7mm) sawn lath. You will need 13 of these but it is best to mill a couple of extra to allow for any failures during the steaming process , .

Place the sawn lath in the steamer for about one and a half hours, keeping the laths apart so that the steam can immerse the fibres (see page 182 for more information about steam-bending equipment and the process).

Take the 26in (66cm) x 2¹/₂in (63mm) length of chestnut and mark a central line down its length by pinging a chalk line. Using the chainsaw carving disc on the angle grinder, cut out a slot that one end of the each lath will fit into. The chainsaw carving disc is a useful tool but must be treated with respect ⑤. If you feel uncomfortable with using it, I advise to make two ripsaw cuts along the chestnut and then chisel out the slot for the laths. A ferret could be useful for cleaning out the slot. Then drill and fix the chestnut pole to the foot ends of the upper side rails, making sure the slot is positioned so that it runs parallel with the direction of the seat.

Take the laths from the steamer one at a time. Quickly slide one end into the slot in the chestnut log and then fix it to the second seat cross stretcher, again to the remaining cross stretchers and then fix it onto the middle back stretcher before finishing behind the bow back. I use silicon bronze ring shanks and always pre-drill holes. Start with the centre lath and work out evenly to each side. Leave the outside (non-steamed) laths for now.

Bend the steam-bent arms around a curved former. I took the shape from an old Victorian bench and curved the arms to it, they measured 30in (76cm) in length. Let them cool for 30 minutes and then transfer them to the seat, tucking the lower part of the arm behind the eighth chestnut seat cross stretcher (counting from the foot of the seat). Drill and fix in place, then drill and fix the other end of the arm to the top bar. Slot two non-steamed pieces of sawn lath into the chestnut slot at the foot of the lounger on each side and fix so that it meets the bottom of the curve of the arm, becoming the outside lath ⑥. Finish the lounger with natural UV protection oil for added weather resistance.

A mobile sawmill converting the sweet chestnut log.

The sawn laths clamped and ready for their final cut.

Chainsaw carving disc on an angle grinder – note the warning cone!

The finished steam-bent sweet chestnut lounger.

LADDER-BACK
ROCKING CHAIR

The ladder back is a traditional rocking chair that falls under the category of post-and-rung construction and is well suited to using hand tools and green wood. Its simplicity and crafted shape ensures a beautiful, yet highly functional, object made from one coppiced log. This project is precise and more complex than many others in this book. The end result is a crafted chair of classic design assembled with no glues or metal fixings.

Meet the Maker

Richard Bates

Richard Bates, who has been refining his chair-making skills, runs a number of courses on making a chair directly from the trees in the woods. Richard learnt coppice management and basic craft skills as an apprentice at Prickly Nut Wood, but it was his time the following summer spent working as Mike Abbott's assistant that opened his eyes to the possibilities of chair making.

"Ash grows super straight. It is a beautiful tree with strong wood that is easy to work and cleave, it behaves well for chair making. All the bits that go wrong make decorative firewood. What I like about chair making is that it is all done in the woods. Using a few simple and a few more specialist tools, the whole process is done in the woods. Firewood provides heat and rainwater for steam bending, no glues are involved. You don't need to go to the hardware store and that's pretty special these days. It is inspiring seeing people who have never worked with wood at all evolve from never having used any tools to turning out an amazing, beautiful chair."

The results of a chair-making course with Mike Abbott.

Richard Bates amongst his woods.

Materials you will need

1 log: 6ft (1.8m) long x 6–8in (150–200mm) diameter
Wych elm bast for weaving the seat: 33yd (30m)
Teak oil

The log will provide:

2 back legs: 43$^{5}/_{16}$in (110cm) long x 1$^{1}/_{2}$in (38mm) diameter
2 front legs: 22$^{7}/_{16}$in (57cm) long x 1$^{1}/_{2}$in (38mm) diameter
2 arms: 19$^{11}/_{16}$in (50cm) long x 3$^{5}/_{32}$in (8cm) wide (then shaped)
5 back slats: 19$^{11}/_{16}$in (50cm) long x 3$^{5}/_{32}$in (8cm) wide (these
will need to be measured and adjusted for your particular
chair as each slat is different. The measurement given will
suffice for the largest slat).
2 front rungs and 1 front seat rail: 19$^{11}/_{16}$in (50cm) long
x 1$^{3}/_{16}$in (30mm) diameter (they will be shaved down from
these measurements)
2 side and 1 back rung and 2 side and 1 back rail:
14$^{61}/_{64}$in (38cm) long x 1$^{3}/_{16}$in (30mm) diameter (they will
be shaved down from these measurements)
2 rockers shaped from a plank: 31$^{1}/_{2}$in (80cm) long
x 6in (15cm) wide

Richard's preferred wood for chair making is ash, and this
seems to be fairly universal amongst the latest generation
of greenwood chair makers. There are many choices for the
material to weave the seat with (see box on page 188).

Recommended tools

Chainsaw, wedges, froe, shaving horse, cleaving brake,
draw knife, spokeshave, axe, hammer, concave spokeshave,
calipers, $^{5}/_{8}$in (16mm) tenon cutter, cordless drill, selection
of auger bits, steam-bending box and jigs for back slats
and legs, gauntlets, chutney trousers vice (see page 184),
mortise chisel, bevelled chisel, ferret, jigsaw, elasticized
bungee cord, Japanese rip saw, nail centre finder, sliding
bevel, cabinet scrapers.

Cleaving and shaping the components

The ideal tree is about 6–8in (150–200mm) diameter and fast
grown $\textcircled{1}$. It needs to be fairly straight but the arms of the
chair can follow the grain if there is a slightly curved section.
Cross cut the stem and cleave the different components from
the round stem. If making the chair straight away, it can be
cross cut to the required lengths. If storing the wood, cross cut
the lengths longer than needed and leave in the round.

First cleave the log using wedges. Use an axe head to find
the centre and hammer it into the end grain $\textcircled{2}$. This opens
up a split that wedges can then be hammered into and, by
placing one wedge in front of another, the log cleaves into
two $\textcircled{3}$, $\textcircled{4}$. Hammer an axe head into the centre of the end
grain of each half and follow with a wedge in the opening split
to create quarters $\textcircled{5}$.

Mark up a quarter to maximize the number of possible
legs that can be obtained. Richard used a blue ring (cut from a
water pipe), which has an internal diameter of 1$^{1}/_{2}$in (38mm),
the finished size of the legs of the chair $\textcircled{6}$. Sections that
are too small for chair legs can be used to make seat rails and
rungs. Use a froe and cleaving brake (see page 202) to split out
the components from the quarters $\textcircled{7}$, $\textcircled{8}$. As with all cleaving
in a brake, pressure is applied to the thicker part to force the
cleave to return to a central position. The back slats are also
cleft with the froe $\textcircled{9}$, $\textcircled{10}$.

*The felled ash tree:
enough wood to
make a number
of chairs. One 6ft
(1.8m) section will
suffice for a ladder-
back chair.*

*A wedge is
hammered into
the opening split,
causing the log to
cleave further.*

The log cleaved in two.

The axe head is hammered into the centre of the end grain.

Cleaving the back slats.

Marking up the end grain of the quarter for chair legs.

Cleaving out the legs using a froe and cleaving brake.

Removing the bark can help to see clearly how the split is progressing up the log.

Cleaving the halves into quarters.

Cleft components for the chair, back slats, legs, rungs and rails.

Removing excess with a hand axe.

Shaving the leg to form a cylinder.

Working to the 1¹/₂in (38mm) diameter circle drawn on the end grain.

Using the plastic ring to size the chair leg.

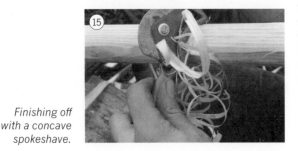

Finishing off with a concave spokeshave.

Work the back legs down to the 1¹/₂in (38mm) ring drawn on the end grain. First remove the excess wood with a small axe (11) and then shave with a draw knife to a cylindrical shape (12), (13). Once the plastic ring can fit over the end grain of the leg it can be used to highlight areas where more shaving is needed (14). Finish the legs with a concave spokeshave (15).

Cleave the seat rails and rungs in the same way as the legs and then cut to length, 19¹¹/₁₆in (50cm) for the front rungs and seat rails and 14⁶¹/₆₄in (38cm) for the back and side seat rails and back and side rungs. If you are working in imperial these measurements can be rounded up or down to the nearest ¹/₈in. The rungs are then shaved down to approximately ⁶/₈in (18–20mm) diameter (16).

Shape the seat rails to the profile of a 'tapered wing' (see picture 19). This involves making the rail approximately ⁶/₈in (20mm) in depth and 1³/₁₆in (30mm) in width. This creates a stronger rail for weaving the seat and dealing with the inward pressure caused by the weave and the weight of the user sitting on the chair. It is critical when shaping the rail to ensure the grain runs with the width of the rail (17). This is critical as the chair will be held together using the oval tenon technique (championed by Mike Abbott). The cross section of a round tenon of green wood will shrink more in one direction than the other. Once it has dried, it will be an oval shape rather than round. The longest section of the oval tenon must go with the grain of the chair leg and not against it, hence the importance of ensuring the grain of the tenon runs with the width of the seat rail.

Checking the rung diameter with a set of calipers.

The grain of the seat rail must run with the width as shown.

Shaving the back slats with a draw knife.

Chair components from top to bottom: cleft back leg blank, cleft and shaven back leg, cleft back-slat blank, cleft and shaven back slat, cleft seat rail or rung blank, cleft and shaven seat rail (note tapered wing shape), cleft and shaven rung.

A manual alternative to the tenon cutter is a hollow shoulder plane.

A tenon cutter attached to a cordless drill cutting a level tenon.

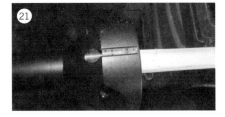

Rung and seat rail with the tenons cut.

Richard's purpose-built drying oven.

Cleave the back slats out with a froe and then work with a draw knife on the shaving horse until they are approximately $5/16$in (8mm) thick . They will be further shaped and finished after they have been steam bent. You should now have the following components: cleft back leg blank, cleft and shaven back leg, cleft back-slat blank, cleft and shaven back slat, cleft seat rail or rung blank, cleft and shaven seat rail, cleft and shaven rung ⑲.

Cut the tenons on the seat rails and rungs using a $5/8$in (16mm) tenon cutter (or a hollow shoulder plane if you prefer a manual alternative ⑳). The tenon cutter is set to a depth of 1in (25mm). To ensure a straight cut with the tenon cutter, the rung or rail must be clamped in a level vice. There is also a level on the tenon cutter to ensure you are not 'wandering off' while cutting ㉑.

Once cut ㉒, dry them for 36–48 hours in a warm environment at about 122–140°F (50–60°C). This could be above a wood-burning stove, in an airing cupboard, in a purpose-built drying oven ㉓ or in a greenhouse. It is important that the temperature remains fairly constant and doesn't get too hot. When they have dried they will have created an oval tenon of approximately $19/32$ x $35/64$in (15 x 14mm). The mortises will be drilled later at $35/64$in (14mm). If the tenons haven't shrunk down to this size, Richard recommends using a $9/16$in (14.3mm) auger. It is useful to have both metric and imperial-sized augers to allow for slight variations. Alternatively, the tenons can be shaved down with a knife to work with the auger sizes you have.

The steamer in operation.

The arms of the jig are lifted, ready to insert the steamed legs.

The arms have bent the legs to the former and a block is clamped in place, so that the arms can be released.

Steam bending the legs and back slats

There are many different designs for steamers but the key function is to boil water and saturate the fibres of the wood by passing steam through a box or tube containing the wood. I have made steamers using army water boilers with laundry hose pipes leading into a custom-made tube. I have also seen steam bending carried out in workshops using an electrical wallpaper stripper to generate the steam. Richard has used a 45-gallon (205 litre) drum. The design is simple. The drum sits on bricks and a fire is built underneath it. The top has been cut off with an angle grinder and a piece of marine plywood is used to make a lid. Holes are made to allow the steam to pass through the marine ply lid. The steam box, also made of marine plywood to the chosen size of the project, sits on top of the lid with holes drilled that line up with the holes in the marine plywood lid. As the water boils in the drum, the steam passes through the steam box, steaming the chair legs and back slats inside and then escaping through the joins in the box (24).

Steam the back legs for one hour, take them out of the steamer (wearing gauntlets – they will be hot!) and clamp them into a steaming jig. This jig is designed to shape the legs to create the ergonomic design that makes the ladder-back chair both aesthetically pleasing and very comfortable. Lift the arms of the jig high (25) and pass the steamed legs under the bar of the jig and slide them under the N-shaped 'henge'. Pull the arms down, which forces the legs to follow the curve of the former. Clamp a block in place to hold the legs in their new position against the former, allowing the arms of the jig to be released (26). Insert wedges under the 'henge' to secure the bottom of the legs to the shape of the former (27), (28). Leave the legs in the jig until they are at least cool to touch, preferably longer, but if you are making multiple chairs and need to keep using the jig, then they can be transferred to a setting jig (29).

The back slats need about 30 minutes in the steamer. Wearing gauntlets, place them in the vice jig and clamp them up (30), (31). They should be left in the vice jig until they have thoroughly cooled and then transferred to the setting jig to dry out (32). The steaming process goes a long way towards seasoning the wood as the steam drives out the sap, so they should dry fairly quickly. Steam the front legs for one hour and then place them in the vice jig with one of the 'half moon' curves taken out, this gives them a slight kick at the top (33).

FAR LEFT: Wedges are inserted beneath the 'henge'.

LEFT: Showing the profile of the former that creates the leg shape.

ABOVE: The legs placed in a setting jig.

CENTRE: The vice jig awaiting the steamed back slats.

FAR RIGHT: The vice jig with the steamed back slats clamped in place.

FAR LEFT: The back slats transferred to the setting jig.

LEFT: The front legs are steam bent to give a slight kick at the top.

The back legs
are clamped
over the bending
former prior
to drilling.

Making up the side frames

Lay the back legs out on the former and clamp them into position ㉞. Measure out the mortise positions using the measurements shown in ㉟. Mark the exact position with a nail centre finder, which is pushed against an oak angle block set at 60 degrees ㊱. Pilot drill a hole, lining up the drill with the oak angle block by eye to get the 60-degree angle ㊲. Finally, drill out the mortise using a $^{35}/_{64}$in (14mm) auger. Notice the use of the angle block to get the 60-degree angle and the insulating tape around the auger to make sure that you don't drill too deep ㊳. Set the angle block to 90 degrees to drill the mortises in the front legs and repeat the process ㊴.

Chamfer the tenons on the rungs and seat rails to ensure a smooth entrance into the mortise ㊵. The seat rail will already have the grain aligned from your caution when making them. The rungs, which could fit into the mortise in any position, will need to align with the oval tenon so that the longest section goes with the grain of the chair leg and not against it. The assembly involves a sash clamp, attached to a work bench with 'chutney trousers' wrapped around the ends of the clamp ㊶. The 'chutney trousers' consist of old clothes and sticky tape to soften the clamps so that neither the frame or the end of the tenon is damaged. By being padded, they compensate for pressure applied against the slightly angled leg of the chair. Insert the tenon into the mortise and wind up the sash clamp ㊷. The creaking noise made is impressive for such small-diameter timber ㊸. Once both the seat rail and rung are attached to one rear leg, offer up the components to the front legs and squeeze together with the sash clamp. Repeat the process for the second side frame ㊹.

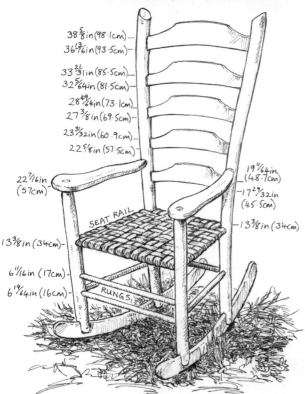

38$\frac{5}{8}$in (98·1cm) —
36$\frac{13}{16}$in (93·5cm) —
33$\frac{21}{31}$in (85·5cm) —
32$\frac{5}{64}$in (81·5cm) —
28$\frac{49}{64}$in (73·1cm) —
27$\frac{3}{8}$in (69·5cm) —
23$\frac{3}{32}$in (60·9cm) —
22$\frac{5}{8}$in (57·5cm) —

22$\frac{7}{16}$in (57cm) —

SEAT RAIL

19$\frac{11}{64}$in (48·7cm) —
17$\frac{29}{32}$in (45·5cm) —
13$\frac{3}{8}$in (34cm) —

13$\frac{3}{8}$in (34cm) —

6$\frac{11}{16}$in (17cm) —
6$\frac{19}{64}$in (16cm) —

RUNGS

㉟ Measurements for the ladder-back rocker taken with zero as the bottom of the chair leg before adding the rockers.

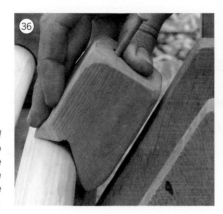

Using a nail
centre finder to
mark the centre
of a mortise with
a 60-degree
angle block.

Using a cordless
drill and angle
block to pilot drill
the mortise.

LEFT: *Drilling out the mortise, lining up the 60-degree angle block by eye.*

CENTRE: *Drilling out the front-leg mortises, lining up the 90-degree angle block by eye.*

BELOW: *A chamfered tenon prior to inserting into the mortise.*

The sash clamp bench with 'chutney trousers'.

Squeezing the tenon into the mortise.

Close-up of the inserted tenon.

The two side frames completed.

Raising the rear leg prior to drilling out mortises into the side frames.

Drilling out the mortises into the side frame.

The edge of one tenon is removed, allowing the seat rails to lock together within the mortise.

Tools for cutting the back-slat mortise; a ferret, a bevelled chisel and a mortise chisel.

Using the sliding bevel to find the steam-bent angle of the back slat.

Drilling mortises for the seat rails and back slats

The next stage is to join the frames together using the seat rails, rungs and the back slats. Due to the trapezoid shape of the seat, the front is wider than the back, so to drill for the front and back seat rails and rungs the back leg must be raised about 2in (50mm) and clamped onto a flat work surface (45). Drill out the mortises for the front and back seat rails (46). This should take out the edge of the tenon of the already fitted side seat rails (47). This slight locking of the tenons should help strengthen the joint.

Next, cut the mortises for the back slats. You will need a ferret, a bevelled chisel and a mortise chisel (48). Mark up the back legs to show the positions of the back-slat mortises. Take the angle of the back slat using a sliding bevel, which then becomes the angle guide for marking and drilling out the mortises (49). Use a nail centre finder and the sliding bevel to transfer the angle to the chair leg (50). Mark out a groove with a chisel to show where to drill the worm (51), (52). Drill out the worm using a $^{15}/_{64}$in (6mm) auger bit (53). Cut the mortise out using a mortise chisel (54) and a bevelled chisel (55), and then clean it out with a ferret (56). This should leave a clean mortise, approximately $^{25}/_{32}$in (20mm) deep (57).

LEFT: Using a nail centre finder and the sliding bevel to transfer the angle for cutting the mortise to the chair leg.

CENTRE: Using a chisel to mark out a groove for drilling out the mortises.

RIGHT: The finished groove, known as a worm.

ABOVE: Drilling out the mortise with an auger bit, following the worm and using the sliding bevel to get the right angle.

CENTRE: Using the mortise chisel to get a straight $^{15}/_{64}$in (6mm) end to the mortise.

FAR RIGHT: Using the bevelled chisel to cut the edge of the mortise.

ABOVE: Removing the cut-away wood with the ferret.

RIGHT: The finished back-slat mortise.

With the dummy rungs in place, the exact length of the back slats can be measured.

Richard lines up the back slats prior to squeezing the chair tightly together.

The frame of the chair fitted together.

Hammering a square peg into a round hole.

The back slat pegged. Over time the leg will shrink tighter around the seasoned oak peg.

Joining the side frames together

Place some dummy rungs and rails in the positions of the actual front and back seat rails and rungs. The dummies should be exactly the same length as the actual rungs and seat rails but the tenons should be a lot thinner so that they easily slide into the mortises. Hold the chair frame together with some elasticized bungee cord so that it is possible to measure from mortise to mortise to get the exact size of the back slats (58). Remember to add on $1^{37}/_{64}$in (40mm), the depth of the two mortises, to your measurement. If you wish to increase the angle of splay of the back of the chair, this can be done by reducing the length of the lower rear rung.

Use a template to draw the shapes onto the back slats (as shown in picture 60) and work them with a draw knife to get the finished pattern. The edges of the back slats should be angle cut where they go into the mortises to match the splay of the back of the chair. Squeeze the front of the chair together. Fit the back rungs, seat rail and the back slats into one side of the mortises and, once it is all lined up (59), squeeze the chair together using the sash clamp with 'chutney trousers' (60). Peg the top back slat to lock the chair together. Richard used a bit of seasoned oak and made a $^{11}/_{64}$in (4.5 mm) square peg that he then hammered into a $^{13}/_{64}$in (5mm) round mortise (61), (62).

MATERIAL FOR SEAT WEAVING

There is a wide choice of material for seat weaving such as rushes, Danish cord, seagrass and shaker tape. But, as I am focusing on woodland crafts, what could be better than the bast (inner bark) from the tree itself? In the US, hickory is a traditional material for seat weaving. In the UK, wych elm is the preferred type of bast and produces a lovely seat looking as if it has been woven with leather. Other basts suitable for seat weaving are western red cedar, lime, and I have one ex-apprentice who weaves his seats with sweet chestnut bast. There are no doubt other possibilities but some I have tried, such as larch, do not have the strength to make a secure seat.

Coils of dried wych elm bast ready to be soaked prior to weaving.

Weaving the seat

The process of harvesting bast involves felling the tree in spring when the sap is flowing and carefully removing the outer bark with a draw knife. Score the bast with a knife down the length of the trunk and then score another line parallel to the first about 1in (25mm) away from it. You can now lift the bast away and roll it up. Rolls of 16–20ft (5–6m) in length are a useful size for weaving. Store the rolls and then soak them in warm water for a few hours prior to weaving to soften them into a flexible fibrous material .

The first tie. The bast is secured to the corner of the rear seat rail to begin weaving the warp.

Tie the bast to the corner of the rear seat rail . Keeping a good tension, bring the bark under the front seat rail and round over the top of it and then back over the rear seat rail and round under it and back under the front seat rail 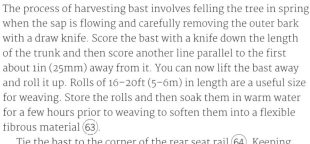. Continue this pattern until the whole seat area is filled. This is known as the warp. There will be gaps where the trapezoid shape of the seat flares out; these will be dealt with at the end.

Filling up the seat with the warp.

There will be a number of occasions when the coil of bark runs out and you will need to join another to it. This is always carried out on the underside of the seat using a weaver's knot. First cut away the width of the existing length of bark to leave a thinner end. Do the same with the end of the new length of bark. Fold both of these thinner ends back on themselves to form two loops. Insert one loop through the other  and then take the thin end of the outer loop and take it back under itself and pass this end through the inner loop. Pull the thick ends in opposite directions to tighten .

Both ends are made into loops, the first stage of the weaver's knot.

Tying the weaver's knot.

Domestic crafts **189**

Once the whole seat area is filled with the warp, you should find that you are near the other opposite back leg from where you started. Take the end of the bast and bring it over the rear seat rail in the corner and then tight around the inside of the back leg and under the side seat rail. The bast can now be brought over the side seat rail and you can begin to weave the weft. For this seat Richard chose a herringbone pattern. As you bring the bast over the side rail you begin the pattern of 'over two strips of the warp and then under two' . For the next row offset the pattern by one. Go 'over one and then under two', and then continue 'over two and under two'. Continue offsetting each row by one strip of the warp. When the weft is complete, there will be small gaps due to the trapezoid shape at each side. You will have some short offcuts of bast from where you have cut back a length to join two pieces on the underside of the chair. Take these and fill in the gaps, following the pattern. The bast will shrink tight as it dries and can be oiled, leaving a natural leather look to the seat ⑥⑨.

Beginning the weft, 'over two, under two'.

Fitting the arms and rockers

Cleave the arms out and then make stopper cuts on the inside of the curves. This can then be axed to shape and finished with a draw knife.

You now have the complication of needing a tenon and a mortise in the same piece of green wood. The tenon will need to be dried out, so that when it is squeezed into the chair leg, the back leg will shrink tightly around it. Meanwhile, the mortise will be fitting onto a tenon on the end of the front leg and the mortise will need to shrink tightly around that. The answer is to dry the bottom end of the arm and keep a bag tight around the upper end to restrict the drying-out process. Cut the tenon down to ⅝in (16mm) with the tenon cutter and drill the mortise out at the other end of the arm, to the same dimensions. The arm drops down about 1½in (38mm) from the front to the back of the chair, so put a 1½in (38mm) block under the front end of the arm before drilling the mortise to ensure the right angle for the tenon. Squeeze the arm so that the tenon fits securely into the mortise in the rear leg. Ripsaw the tenon on the front leg using a fine Japanese saw the depth of the thickness of the arm. Squeeze the arm onto the tenon and wedge it with a seasoned oak wedge ⑦⓪ .

Shape the rockers out of a cleaved ash plank using stopper cuts ⑦①. For this particular chair Richard used a seasoned oak plank and cut the rockers out using a jigsaw. This is sensible as the oak plank was air dried and therefore the legs will shrink tightly around it. If the chair is to be used on a veranda, the extra durability of the oak will help preserve the chair for longer. Another cyclical part of this chair is that the oak plank was one that Richard milled with me during his time at Prickly Nut Wood. Where possible, a curved plank where the grain follows a similar pattern to the shape of the rockers should be chosen.

The completed woven seat.

Detail of the front leg tenon through the arm mortise with oak wedge.

Axing out a rocker using stop cuts.

Fitting the rockers.

The completed
ladder-back
rocking chair.

To fit the rockers to the chair, the four legs should be levelled first. Next, with the chair upside down, lay the rocker over the bottom of the legs and mark its width. The finished rocker width should be about ⁵/₈in (16mm). Measure 1³/₁₆in (30mm) down from the rocker and mark the back and front of each leg. The curve of the rocker will mean the distances on each side of each leg will be different. Drill through each leg using a ⁵/₈in (16mm) auger bit. Then, using a Japanese rip saw, saw down

the lines you have drawn on the bottom of the chair legs to meet the drilled hole. This will leave each leg with an inverted 'U' shape at the bottom. Offer the rockers and make any minor adjustments. Drill a ¹³/₆₄in (5mm) mortise hole and hammer in a square oak peg of ¹¹/₆₄in (4.5mm) ⑦②.

Finally, clean up the chair with cabinet scrapers and then finish with a coat of oil. Richard used teak oil on the chair and seat. Sit back, relax and enjoy the rocking motion ⑦③.

Craft materials in development. Three-year-old sweet chestnut, showing the abundance of available stems in a well-managed coppice.

TOOLS AND DEVICES
FOR WOODLAND CRAFTS

Tools

TOP: A long-handled carpenter's adze.
CENTRE: Hollowing adze.
BOTTOM: Cleaving adzes.

TOP: A selection of bar augers.
BOTTOM: 'Woodowl' bit.

ABOVE: Side axes come in left-and right-handed patterns.

ABOVE: A selection of billhooks.

TOP: A brace with a Jennings pattern bit.
BOTTOM: Calipers.

Adzes

These come in many shapes and sizes. The main ones used in green woodworking are the carpenter's adze with a long dog-legged handle for standing over the timber and working it down closer to the finished shape. A smaller curved adze with a short handle is used for hollowing chair seats and a cleaving adze with a straighter blade is used for cleaving timber. I have different-sized cleaving adzes and use the small Sussex adze for cleaving thin rods for making woven fencing panels.

Augers

Bar or scotch-eye augers are useful where a slow, carefully drilled hole is needed. I have a large 2in (50mm) bar auger, which I use for legs on shaving horses and other rustic furniture. Modern auger bits, which are used in power drills, vary considerably in quality. The Japanese 'woodowl' bits are the most superior I use and are the only auger bits I would recommend for timber-framing work.

Axes

These come in many shapes and styles but it is the side axe that I use the most for craft work. With a bevel on one side, they come in left- or right-handed versions and are excellent for preparing a flat face on a cleft piece of wood.

Billhooks

These come in many patterns, often with regional significance where a particular trade was plentiful. I use billhooks for cutting short-rotation coppice, hedge laying and snedding up brash. They are used for cleaving, especially by hurdle makers, and are a universally useful woodland tool.

Brace and bit

These are traditional hand drills with a range of different patterns of bit, now mainly superseded by cordless drills. Like the bar auger, they are still useful because of the control and slow speed of cut they produce. I mainly use Jennings pattern bits.

Calipers

This is a precise measuring tool. Once you start using one, you find endless uses for it. Very useful when chair making for checking tenon thickness and shrinkage.

TOP: *A selection of carpenter's squares.*

BOTTOM: *Chain carving disc.*

ABOVE: *Electric chain mortiser.*

TOP: *Chalk line with container of chalk.*

BOTTOM: *Chalk line being used on a roundwood pole to centralize a tenon.*

ABOVE: *Framing chisels.*

TOP: *A selection of clamps.*

BOTTOM: *De-barking spade.*

Carpenter's square

Used for measuring right angles, the carpenter's square has a multitude of uses, particularly in timber framing.

Carving disc

This is a modern tool that attaches to an angle grinder with a small chainsaw chain spinning around a 4in (100mm) disc. It is very effective for roughing out bowls and troughs and for cutting narrow slots in timber. However, keeping detailed control with the tool takes practice and I would warn any user to take the greatest of care.

Chain mortiser

A power tool that has a bar with a wide cutting chain. It is used in timber framing and post-and-rail fencing.

Chalk line

This is a string line that is coiled in a case of coloured chalk. It is very useful for creating a straight line by stretching the string and then lifting the centre and releasing. I use these a lot in roundwood timber framing.

Chisels

There are a wide range of chisels used in woodworking but the main type I use are framing chisels. These are heavy-duty chisels, which can be struck with a maul and are used in cutting the joints on a timber frame. (See also turning chisels, gouges and slicks.)

Clamps

These come in a variety of shapes and sizes. They are used when steam bending for holding steam-bent wood to a former and larger sash clamps are used for windows and doors.

De-barking spade

A long-handled tool used for removing the bark from logs. Used regularly in roundwood timber framing.

TOP: *Dog-leg gouge.*
BOTTOM: *Draw knife.*

TOP: *Electric drill.*
BOTTOM: *Cordless battery drill.*

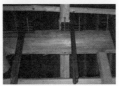

TOP: *Ferret.*
CENTRE: **Yurt crown** *former.*
BOTTOM: *A selection of framing pins.*

TOP: *From left to right: shingling froe, cleaving froe and lath froe.*
BOTTOM: *Framing gouges.*

TOP: *Hollow shoulder planes.*
BOTTOM: *Hooked carving knife.*

Dog-leg gouge

This is a specialized tool used in carving for hollowing out troughs and bowls.

Draw knife

Another green woodworking 'must have' tool. The draw knife is used for peeling and reducing timber. Often used in conjunction with a shaving horse, they come in many shapes and sizes. Bevelled on one side, they can peel large poles or be used for detailed work on a chair leg.

Drills

Cordless drills have improved considerably over the past few years and I use one regularly in much of my work. A power drill with high torque is the perfect companion for a 'woodowl' auger bit when timber framing.

Ferret

A small, hooked tool used for cleaning out slot mortises in chair making and for creating rings on baby's rattles on the pole lathe, amongst other uses.

Former

A device often made from an existing object or a shape formed from plywood onto which steam-bent wood is clamped to mould its shape.

Framing pins

Metal T-shaped pins, just slightly smaller than the hole drilled through a timber frame. I use these when re-erecting a timber frame (made on a framing bed) in its final position.

Froes

These come in different sizes and thicknesses and are used for cleaving wood. Larger froes are for shingle making and smaller froes are for making laths.

Gouges

Small gouges are used for detailed carving work and larger framing gouges can be used for hollowing out. I use them for cutting the curved scribed profile on a round pole in timber framing.

Hollow shoulder plane

These produce a round tenon with a shoulder and are used in furniture making.

Hooked knife

These are used in spoon carving and are designed to hollow out the curve of the bowl. They are sold in left- or right-handed designs.

TOP: *A cordless impact driver.*

BOTTOM: *A cordless jigsaw.*

ABOVE: *Japanese saws.*

TOP: *A selection of Japanese ceramic water stones.*

BOTTOM: *A selection of levels.*

TOP: *Log dogs.*

BOTTOM: *Two sets of loppers.*

ABOVE: *Applewood mauls.*

Impact driver

A cordless impact driver when used in conjunction with timber locks creates a strong and quick way of drawing timber together. I use one a lot for fitting temporary bracing when raising timber frames and for more permanent fixing in other construction works.

Jigsaw

Jigsaws are used for cutting curves and circles in wood. I used one for the seat in the bar stool project (see page 148).

Japanese saws

Cutting on the pull, rather than the push, the influence of Japanese saws is growing on European craftsmen with good reason. These thin saws cut so cleanly the finish looks as if you have planed the timber. I use them for many applications in craftwork and roundwood timber framing.

Japanese water stones

I use these ceramic stones for sharpening gouges, billhooks, draw knives and spokeshaves, amongst other tools.

Levels

I use spirit levels for many crafts, larger tripod dumpy levels when timber framing and laser levels to show where to cut angled curves in roundwood.

Log dogs

These are used to hold timber secure during timber framing. They have flat spikes at 90 degrees to each other to go with the grain in both logs.

Loppers

These are useful when making woven fencing, panels and hurdles.

Maul

Usually made from one piece of wood, (often fruit woods like apple), a maul is used to strike a framing chisel.

TOP: Minijarn gouge.

BOTTOM: A selection of planes; note the small 'detail rabbet plane'.

TOP: Using a profile gauge on a roundwood framing pole.

BOTTOM: Plumb line being used in a doorway.

TOP: A collection of ratchet straps.

BOTTOM: A selection of different sized rounding planes.

TOP: From the top: battery chainsaw, triangular bow saw, panel saw and folding pruning saw.

BOTTOM: Log scribers being used to scribe a roundwood pole.

TOP: A log-scribing pod in use.

BOTTOM: A slick.

Minijarn gouge
A Scandinavian design for gouging out spoon bowls.

Nug
Another name for a stail engine.

Plane
There are many types and sizes of plane for different crafts. Many woodland crafts have no need of a plane for the timber is in the round or a cleft finish is the desired look. However, where a smoother finish is desirable, like on the seats of the bar stool project (see page 148), a plane can be a useful addition.

Profile gauge
This is used for measuring and transferring the profile of the curve of wood.

Plumb line
A weighted line used to find vertical positions, used a lot in timber framing.

Ratchet straps
Used for tying down and securing large timbers, particularly in roundwood timber framing.

Rounding, or rotary, planes
These are used for creating a tapered end to a round pole. I use them for peg making.

Saws
There are many saws for woodland crafting. I use a bow saw and pruning saw for small-diameter round poles; a battery chainsaw for larger diameters and during roundwood timber framing; and a panel saw for most other work. (See also Japanese saws.)

Scribers
A key tool in roundwood-timber framing and log building. Used to create accurate profile images of other logs and transfer jointing positions. Used for the butterpat joint in the roundwood caravan project (see page 110).

Scribing pod
A simple tool made up of two pieces of welded angle iron, which are used in pairs to lift logs and give more room to scribe.

Slick
Resembling a long-handled chisel but behaving more like a plane, the slick smooths and finishes. I use one regularly when smoothing a flat surface or large tenon during timber framing.

TOP: *A Japanese sliding bevel.*

BOTTOM: *Copper soldering iron.*

TOP: *Stail engine.*

BOTTOM: *A large steamer being used to bend roundwood roof rafters.*

TOP: *A tenon cutter being used on chair stretchers.*

CENTRE: *A pair of carpenter's trestles.*

BOTTOM: *A set of turning chisels.*

TOP: *Workshop vice.*

CENTRE: *Portable vice with spare jaws for gripping round poles.*

BOTTOM: *Twybil.*

TOP: *A water-cooled sharpening machine.*

CENTRE: *A wedge with a twist to encourage cleaving.*

BOTTOM: *Whittling knife.*

Sliding bevel

A sliding bevel is used for setting an angle, which can then be transferred to other pieces of timber.

Soldering irons

These are the old copper soldering irons that are heated up in a fire. They are used to create a square mortise by burning out the corners of a round hole. Used in yurt making.

Stail engine

This is used for creating a tapered pole. It is similar to a rounding plane but with the ability to adjust the taper. Used in stick making and rake handles.

Steamer

There are many types of steamer used for saturating the fibres of green wood with steam in order to change the shape. The steamed wood is clamped to a former and allowed to cool.

Tenon cutter

This is used for creating tenons on small-diameter roundwood. It is used in the ladder-back rocking chair (see page 176) and bar stool (see page 148) projects.

Trestles

These are used for supporting and clamping wood.

Turning chisels

Chisels that are designed for use with a lathe.

Twybil

This is also known as a mortising knife and is used in the manufacture of gate hurdles.

Vice

This is used for clamping timber. I use portable vices as the changeover from sawn wood jaws to roundwood jaws is quick and easy.

Water-cooled sharpening system

A good water-cooled grinding machine makes sharpening quick and accurate. I sharpen all my framing chisels this way.

Wedges

Used for splitting large logs down into smaller components.

Whittling knife

Used in spoon making and carving, these whittling knives are a useful addition.

Devices

Cleaving brake

The cleaving brake is often used in conjunction with a froe for splitting wood down into smaller sections and is a key device used in many of the woodland crafts in this book.

Easel cleaving brake

A simple design of cleaving brake, used commonly in cleaving chestnut for fencing.

Knee vice

This works by pushing the bottom of a cleft plank with your knee. The plank is pivoted so the top closes against a horizontal timber and holds the pole in place to be peeled. A weight opens the vice when pressure from your knee is removed.

Peeling jig

A simple but very effective peeling jig that can be adjusted to take long poles.

Pole lathe

Historically the device of chair bodgers and bowl turners, the pole lathe produces finished pieces as well as components for making larger projects.

Roundwood peeler

A simple device of my own design, arrived at through peeling many large round poles.

Shake brake

Consisting of different-sized angled slots in a beam, the shake brake allows the maker some control of the cleave as the block gets smaller.

Shaving horse

This must be the most used woodland craft device. The timber is clamped in a vice by pushing forwards with your legs, and the seated craftsman can use a draw knife to shave down the wood. Many adaptations of the basic model have been developed for different crafts.

Woodsman's grip

A simple device used for bundling wood, in particular when making faggots.

AN EXTRA PAIR OF HANDS

Devices (sometimes referred to as 'an extra pair of hands') have developed throughout history in association with particular crafts. Many, such as the shaving horse, pole lathe and cleaving brake, are now fairly universal, with some regional or particular craft variations. Others are more unusual and many are invented by a woodsman for a particular task only to be left where they were made decaying in the woods, never to be passed on to others. The devices here are a selection, but step-by-step details of how to make them, and others, is the subject of another book.

Triangulated cleaving brake.

Easel cleaving brake.

Forked knee vice.

Sussex knee vice.

Peeling jig.

Shake brake.

Pole lathe.

Roundwood peeler.

Classic shaving horse.

Shaving horse frame.

Dumbhead shaving horse.

Mike Abbott's shaving horse 2000.

Woodsman's grip.

The future

Forty years ago the future for traditional woodland crafts and its associated woodsmanship looked bleak. The craftsmen were an ageing population and those entering the industry were few and far between. However, 40 years on and the outlook is changing for the better.

At the time of writing this, there are a number of regional coppice groups in the UK, some with an active membership and a National Coppice Federation to represent the industry. Apprenticeships are returning and the Bill Hogarth Memorial Apprenticeship Trust has been running a three-year apprenticeship for a number of years now. Many of its participants are actively working in the industry, particularly in the Cumbria region. Support through the Ernest Cook Trust and some successful crowd-funding campaigns have helped keep a small but steady flow of new faces entering the industry.

My own scheme in Sussex, supported by the charity Woodland Heritage, has produced a number of new entrants into the industry with, at the last count, 15 now working in the coppice and greenwood industry with some specializing in timber framing. Other individuals such as Mike Abbott in Herefordshire have been producing young craftsmen skilled in the techniques of chair making and associated crafts that he has carefully refined. Added to this, the growth in forest schools is, at last, enabling children in the education system to taste the wonders of what our woodlands have to offer. Who knows how many may choose the route of a woodland lifestyle when touched by its essence at an early age? The growth and fascination in whittling spoons is on the increase: for many it is their first taste of working with green wood and may lead to a desire to discover more. So, overall the picture is a lot brighter than 40 years ago.

However, there are still areas that need to be addressed. The management of the coppice resource is key to all the woodland crafts and associated industry and is the area that needs addressing the most. Derelict coppice needs restoration, young growing coppice needs protection from deer and on-cycle coppice needs continued management. Making the woodland crafts brings high levels of satisfaction but the long-term management of the resource is the legacy that continues.

I have been cutting coppice at Prickly Nut Wood for 23 years now. I began with eight acres (3.24 hectares), and have increased the area I manage, taking on the management of surrounding derelict coppice, to 80 acres (32.4 hectares). Restoring woodland in a poor condition, overrun with rhododendron, can seem like a thankless task but gradually, year upon year the progress can be clearly seen. Each year, I now cut short-rotation as well as derelict coppice and some areas I have now cut four times. The biodiversity is increasing, butterfly populations are growing and the quality of the coppice poles from which to make the crafts is improving. Looking after the coppice resource with care and good management is key to the woodland craft industry.

The other key area to be addressed is the futures market. By this, I mean obtaining outlets and designing new products. If the industry is to grow and our coppice woodlands to become restored, we need some new markets to drive the industry. An ex-apprentice of mine, Max Lyne is designing lamps made from sweet chestnut coppice, and it is products like these that may play an important role in seeing woodland craft products make their way to a wider market and help educate the public about coppice systems and sustainable woodland management.

The future, as always, is uncertain but well-managed coppice woodlands and a young generation empowered with the techniques to make crafts from the materials around them bodes well for a time when the production lines of plastic replicas of wooden crafts comes to a standstill. It is from the woods and the long-term thinking that goes hand in hand with their stewardship that a healthy and sustainable society will return.

Glossary

Bast
Phloem, the fibrous inner bark of a tree used for seat weaving.

Bender
A temporary home or shelter made from hazel branches with a canvas covering, used commonly in woodlands.

Binders
Twisted binding between stakes on a laid hedge, usually hazel. Also called 'etherings'.

Bodger
The name for craftsmen who make chair legs on a pole lathe.

Bole
The main stem up to the first branch of a tree.

Box frame
A term used to describe a form of construction where the building is framed out of horizontal and vertical timbers to produce a wooden box.

Brash
Small branches from the side and top of trees.

Broadleaf tree
Any tree that has broad leaves rather than needles.

Burr
A rough growth that develops on a tree.

Butterpat joint
A scribed joint that resembles a pat of butter in a dish, often where the cruck meets the tie-beam on a roundwood timber frame.

Cambium layer
Plant tissue layer between the inner bark and the wood.

Cant
A defined area of coppice, also regionally referred to as 'panel'.

Chutney trousers
The name given to padding over the metal parts of a sash clamp, usually consisting of tape and old clothing used in compressing a chair joint.

Cleave
To split unsawn timber by forcing the fibres apart along its length.

Clump
A small group of trees.

Coppice
Broadleaf trees cut during the dormant season, which produce continual multi-stems that are harvested for wood products.

Coupe
A clear felled area of woodland, sometimes coppice.

Crown
The branches and top of a tree above the bole, also the circular hoop at the top of a yurt.

Cruck
A primitive truss formed by two main timbers, usually curved, set up as an arch or inverted V.

Faggot
A tied bundle of small branches traditionally used to fire ovens, now used for river bank restoration and coastal defence.

Glade
A clearing within the woodland.

Greenwood
Freshly cut, unseasoned wood.

In-cycle coppice
Coppice that has been cut at regular intervals and is not overstood.

Lath
Thin cleft strips of wood used primarily for a framework in a wall upon which plaster (traditionally lime) is applied.

Layering
Pegging down a living stem to make it root and create another tree.

Lop and top
See Brash.

Maiden
A single-stem tree that has not been coppiced.

Mast year
A year when trees produce a large amount of seed.

Mortise
A chiselled slot into, or through, which a tenon is inserted.

Noggin
Horizontal timber braces between floor joists or studwork to add strength and rigidity to the construction.

Oigg
A Sussex word for capping on a gate post.

Overstood coppice
Coppice that has not been cut for many years and is out of rotation for usual coppice produce.

Ping
The process when a chalked string is stretched and manually released to mark a length of timber.

Pollard
A tree that has been cut above grazing animal height to allow repeated harvesting of poles from the crown.

Rive
See cleave.

Scribing
To mark a timber by scratching or drawing a line.

Snedding
The removal of side branches and top of a felled tree.

Stail
A long wooden handle, for example in rake making.

Standard
A single-stemmed tree allowed to grow to maturity, commonly amongst coppice.

Stool
The stump of a coppiced tree from which new stems grow, also a simple seat.

Suckering
Re-growth from existing roots of a tree after cutting.

Tenon
The projecting end of a timber that is inserted into a mortise.

Underwood
Coppiced woodland.

Yurt
A wooden-framed transportable dwelling with canvas covering, originating from Asia and now found more regularly as a dwelling in woodlands.

Zale
Upright poles around which other poles are woven. Typically used for hurdles.

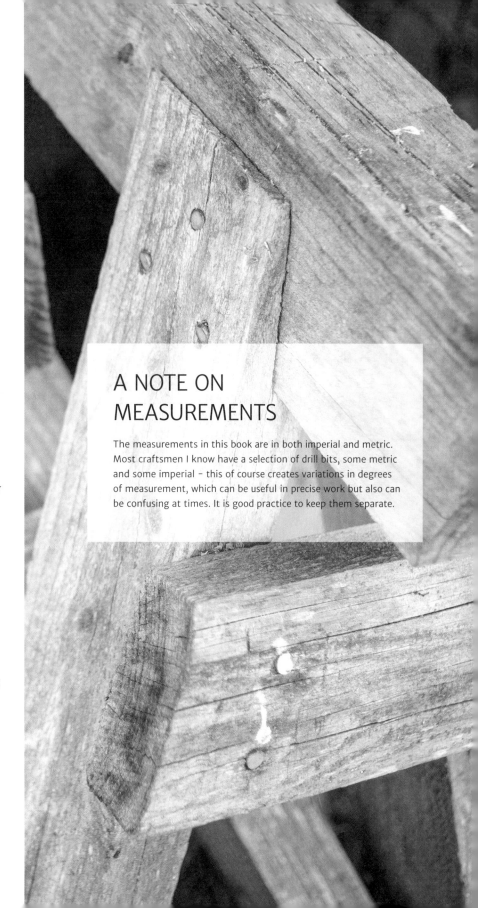

A NOTE ON MEASUREMENTS

The measurements in this book are in both imperial and metric. Most craftsmen I know have a selection of drill bits, some metric and some imperial – this of course creates variations in degrees of measurement, which can be useful in precise work but also can be confusing at times. It is good practice to keep them separate.

Resources

Further reading

Ancient Woodland by Oliver Rackham (Castlepoint Press, 1980) The definitive text on ancient woodland.

Carving and Whittling, the Swedish Style by Gert Ljungberg and Inger Ason-Ljungberg (Lark Books, 1999)

Collins Guide to Tree Planting & Cultivation by H. Edlin (Collins, 1975) Recommended guide.

Complete Practical Book of Country Crafts by Jack Hill (David & Charles, 1979)

Coppicing and Coppice Crafts by Rebecca Oaks and Edward Mills (The Crowood Press, 2010) Good introduction to coppicing and crafts with Cumbrian flavour.

Country Craft Tools by Percy W. Blandford (Swan Hill Press, 1997)

Flora Britannica by Richard Mabey (Chatto & Windus, 1996) The evolving culture of Britain's flora.

Going with the Grain: Making Chairs in the 21st Century by Mike Abbott (Living Wood Books, 2011) Detailed chair-making book from tree to finished product from one of the country's most experienced chair-making tutors.

Greenwood Crafts: A Comprehensive Guide by Edward Mills and Rebecca Oaks (The Crowood Press, 2012) Excellent complement to their coppicing and coppice crafts book.

Green Woodwork: Working with Wood the Natural Way by Mike Abbott (Guild of Master Craftsman Publications, 1989)

Green Woodworking: A Hands-on Approach by Drew Langster (Lark Books, 1995)

Green Woodworker's Pattern Book by Ray Tabor (Batsford, 2005) An excellent, well-researched pattern book with many craft designs.

History of the Countryside by Oliver Rackham (Phoenix, 2000) A fascinating description of how the British landscape and human activities have interacted over many centuries to create what we see today.

Living Woods: From Buying a Woodland to Making a Chair by Mike Abbott (Living Wood Books, 2013) Mike's journey of working in the woods with practical craftwork.

Make a Chair from a Tree by John D. Alexander, Jr (The Astragal Press, 1994)

Making Rustic Furniture by Daniel Mack (Lark Books, 1990) Inspirational.

Oak-Framed Buildings by Rupert Newman (Guild of Master Craftsman Publications, 2005, revised 2014)

Roundwood Small-diameter Timber for Construction edited by Alpo Ranta-Maunus (VTT Publications, 1999) A report on the structural testing of roundwood.

Roundwood Timber Framing by Ben Law (Permanent Publications, 2010) A 'how to' build with roundwood book.

Sharpening: The Complete Guide by Jim Kingshott (Guild of Master Craftsman Publications, 1994)

The Chairmaker's Workshop by Drew Langster (Lark Books, 1999)

The Complete Book of Basketry Techniques by Sue Gabriel and Sally Goymer (David & Charles, 1991)

The Complete Yurt Handbook by Paul King (Eco-Logic Books, 2001)

The New Sylva by Gabriel Hemery and Sarah Simblet (Bloomsbury, 2014) Beautifully illustrated update on John Evelyn's original work.

The Rustic Furniture Companion: Traditions, Techniques and Inspirations by Daniel Mack (Lark Books, 1996) Further inspiration.

The Woodland House by Ben Law (Permanent Publications, 2005) Building a roundwood sweet chestnut house in a woodland.

The Woodland Way: A Permaculture Approach to Sustainable Woodland by Ben Law (Permanent Publications, 2001, revised and updated 2013) Sustainable woodland management, classic text.

The Woodland Year by Ben Law (Permanent Publications, 2008) A month-by-month guide to working the woods and associated crafts, including entries from other woodland craftsmen.

The Woodwright's Shop: A Practical Guide to Traditional Woodcraft by Roy Underhill (The University of North Carolina Press, 1981)

Timber Building in Britain by R.W. Brunskill (Victor Gollancz, 1985)

Tools and Devices for Coppice Crafts
by F. Lambert (Centre for Alternative
Technology, first published as a Young
Farmers' Club Booklet, 1957)
Hard to read, but many useful designs.

Traditional Country Craftsmen
by J. Geraint Jenkins (Routledge, 1965)

Traditional Woodland Crafts by Raymond
Tabor (Batsford, 1994)
Well illustrated and practical.

*Trees and Woodlands in the British
Landscape: The Complete History of Britain's
Trees, Woods and Hedgerows*
by Oliver Rackham (Weidenfeld & Nicolson,
1995)
Excellent historical perspective.

Woodcolliers and Charcoal Burning
by Lyn Armstrong (Coach Publishing House
Ltd and the Weald and Downland Open Air
Museum, 1978)
A historical, rather than practical,
perspective.

Woodland Crafts in Britain by Herbert L.
Edlin (David & Charles, 1949)
A classic text, now out of print.

*Woodsman: Living in a Wood in the 21st
Century* by Ben Law (Harper Collins, 2013)
My journey to becoming a woodsman.

Periodicals

Agroforestry News
www.agroforestry.co.uk

The Dendrologist
www.dendrologist.org.uk

Fine Woodworking
www.finewoodworking.com

Forestry Journal
www.forestryjournal.co.uk

The Land Magazine
www.thelandmagazine.org.uk

Living Woods Magazine
www.livingwoodsmagazine.co.uk

Permaculture Magazine
www.permaculture.co.uk

Reforesting Scotland
www.reforestingscotland.org

Woodlots
www.woodnet.org.uk

Coppice cooperatives and groups

Coppice Directory
www.coppice-products.co.uk

Coppice Association North West (CANW)
www.coppicenorthwest.org.uk

Cornwall Group
www.sites.google.com/site/
tomkempwoodsman

Cumbria/North Lancashire
www.coppicecoop.co.uk

Dorset Coppice Group
www.dorsetcoppicegroup.co.uk

East Anglian Coppice Network
www.eastangliancoppicenetwork.
wordpress.com

East Midlands Coppice Association
andrew.alder@outlook.com

Gloucestershire Coppice Group
www.westcountrycoppice.co.uk

Hampshire Coppice Group
www.hampshirecoppice.co.uk

Leeds
www.leedscoppiceworkers.co.uk

Malvern Hills Coppice Network
www.malverncoppicing.co.uk

National Coppice Federation
www.ncfed.org.uk

Sussex & Surrey Coppice Group
www.coppicegroup.wordpress.com

Tool suppliers

Ashem Crafts
www.ashemcrafts.com

Ashley Iles (Edge Tools) Ltd
www.ashleyiles.co.uk

Axminster Tools
www.axminster.co.uk

Bristol Design
www.bristol-design.co.uk

Old Tool Store
www.oldtoolstore.com

The Woodsmith Experience
www.woodsmithexperience.co.uk

Woodland Craft Supplies
www.woodlandcraftsupplies.co.uk

Organisations

Association of Polelathe Turners and
Greenwood Workers
www.bodgers.org.uk

The Basketmakers' Association
www.basketassociation.org.uk

Bill Hogarth Memorial Apprenticeship Trust
www.coppiceapprentice.org.uk

Green Wood Centre
www.smallwoods.org.uk

Heritage Crafts Association
www.heritagecrafts.org.uk

Small Woods Association
www.smallwoods.org.uk

Tree Council
www.treecouncil.org.uk

Woodland Heritage
www.woodlandheritage.org

Woodland Trust
www.woodlandtrust.org.uk

Contact list

Craftspeople who have contributed or been
mentioned in this book. (There is a growing
number of coppice workers and greenwood
craftspeople across the UK, check out the
coppice products website and local coppice
groups.)

Alan Waters
Tel: +44 1243 778106
E-mail: wildwoodcoppice@btinternet.com
Charcoal, pimps and hazel products.

Barn Carder
barnthespoon.com
London-based spoon maker. Runs spoon-
making courses at the Green Wood Guild
(thegreenwoodguild.com).

Ben Law
www.ben-law.co.uk
Roundwood-timber framer, teacher, coppicer,
chestnut products in West Sussex.

Claire Godden
Blackbark Woodland Management in the
Yorkshire woods.

Darren Hammerton
Tel: +44 7816 930899
E-mail: darren@out-of-the-woods.co.uk
Hurdles, hedge laying and timber frames in
Hampshire.

Justin Owen
Tel: +44 7876 333427
Lath and chestnut products in Surrey.

Martin Hazell
www.madeinthevale.com
Baskets and spoons.

Max Lyne
www.maximlyne.com
Designer working with coppice wood to
reach new markets.

Mike Abbott
goingwiththegrain.org
Author, chair making and greenwood work
teacher in Herefordshire.

Millar Hammond
www.traditionalgreenwoodcrafts.wordpress.com
Yurt maker in France.

Paul South
www.paulsouthwoodcraft.com
Woodland management, greenwood crafts
and small structures on Exmoor, North
Devon.

Richard Bates
www.greenwoodcreations.co.uk
Chair making and greenwood crafts
on the Sussex/Hampshire border.

Richard Ely
www.greenwoodcraftsman.com
Spoons, chairs and chestnut products
in East Sussex.

"Permaculture offers innovative ways for you to deal with our changing climate and its effect on us all. Taking its inspiration from robust, biodiverse natural systems, it offers practical ways for all of us to live more sustainable, harmonious and productive lives."

permaculture

Ben Law is a regular contributor to *Permaculture: practical solutions for self-reliance*. This bestselling international environmental magazine is packed with inspiring articles written by leading experts alongside readers' own tips and solutions. Published quarterly, this pioneering publication is full of money-saving ideas for your home, garden and community. It features thought-provoking articles on:

· Organic gardening
· Food and drink
· Renewable technology and green building
· Education, health and economics
· Transition towns and ecovillages
· Personal and community development
· Woodlands
· Sustainable agriculture and agroforestry

It is also full of reviews of the latest books, dvds, tools and products, details of courses and access to opportunities that will help you achieve your own goals and dreams.

To subscribe, check daily updates and to sign up to the eNewsletter go to: **www.permaculture.co.uk**

What is permaculture?

Permaculture is an innovative framework for creating sustainable ways of living. It is a practical method of developing ecologically harmonious, efficient and productive systems that can be used by anyone, anywhere.

By thinking carefully about the way we use our resources – food, energy, shelter and other material and non-material needs – it is possible to get much more out of life by using less. We can be more productive for less effort, reaping benefits for our environment and ourselves, for now and for future generations.

This is the essence of permaculture; the design of an ecologically sound way of living, in our households, gardens, woodlands, communities and businesses. It is achieved by cooperating with nature and caring for the earth and its people.

About the author

Ben Law, woodsman, craftsman, eco-builder, teacher and writer, lives and works in Prickly Nut Wood in West Sussex, UK. The building of his unique woodland home was featured on channel 4's Grand Designs in the UK and was voted by viewers as the most popular episode ever. In addition to the coppicing of his own woodland, he runs courses on sustainable woodland management, roundwood timber framing and occasional tours of his woodland and home. He also trains apprentices and makes a range of craft produce, some of which was commissioned for Prince Harry's 'Sentebale' charity garden at The Chelsea Flower Show 2015. Ben is the author of several books; *The Woodland Way* (Permanent Publications, 2001), *The Woodland House* (Permanent Publications, 2005), *The Woodland Year* (Permanent Publications, 2008), *Roundwood Timber Framing* (Permanent Publications, 2011), *Woodsman: Living in a wood in the 21st Century* (HarperCollins, 2013) and *Woodland Workshop* (GMC Publications, 2018).
www.ben-law.co.uk

Acknowledgements

I would like to thank my ongoing inspiration, which is Prickly Nut Wood, my woodland home amidst the deep woods of West Sussex. I would like to thank the many generations of apprentices that have passed through Prickly Nut Wood and in particular Millar Hammond and Paul South who happened to be involved during the time of writing this book and assisted me with some of the projects. A special thanks goes to my friend Martini, who has shared with me the joys of travelling the world without a passport!

Index

To place an order, or to request a catalogue, contact:
GMC Publications Ltd, Castle Place, 166 High Street, Lewes, East Sussex, BN7 1XU, United Kingdom
Tel: +44 (0)1273 488005   www.gmcbooks.com